As one of the world's longest established and best-known travel brands, Thomas Cook are the experts in travel.

For more than 135 years our guidebooks have unlocked the secrets of destinations around the world, sharing with travellers a wealth of experience and a passion for travel.

Rely on Thomas Cook as your travelling companion on your next trip and benefit from our unique heritage.

Thomas Cook **traveller** guides

DUBAI

Diana Darke

Written and updated by Diana Darke
Original photography by Diana Darke

Published by Thomas Cook Publishing
A division of Thomas Cook Tour Operations Limited
Company registration no. 3772199 England
The Thomas Cook Business Park, 9 Coningsby Road,
Peterborough PE3 8SB, United Kingdom
Email: books@thomascook.com, Tel: +44 (0) 1733 416477
www.thomascookpublishing.com

Produced by Cambridge Publishing Management Limited
Burr Elm Court, Main Street, Caldecote CB23 7NU
www.cambridgepm.co.uk

ISBN: 978-1-84848-446-7

Series Editor: Karen Beaulah
Production/DTP: Steven Collins

Printed and bound in Spain by GraphyCems

Cover photography © Reinhard Schmid/Huber/4Corners

Contents

Introduction

It is rare that a destination's fortunes change so dramatically within such a short space of time as Dubai's have in the last couple of years. It seems only yesterday that all the reports were about the emirate defying the sceptics who were prophesying that the construction bubble must burst and that the vision was not sustainable. When the global financial crisis finally hit, Dubai was forced to eat humble pie, but only for a while – it is already fighting back hard.

As recently as summer 2009, Dubai was still protesting that it was unaffected by the world economic downturn. Later that year, however, shock waves hit the world stock markets when it emerged that Dubai had asked for a debt moratorium. Once hailed as an example to all, an economic miracle with unstoppable momentum, the tiny emirate that had monopolised 25 per cent of the world's cranes at the height of its construction frenzy suddenly ran up against the credit crunch. With over 107 per cent of its GDP owed in loans to creditors, 'Creditopolis', as it was dubbed, came tumbling down. The bubble finally burst.

Thanks to the oil wealth discovered in the 1960s, Dubai had fast-forwarded from an 18th-century lifestyle to a 21st-century one in little more than a generation. It invited the world to come and share the vision, tax-free, and they did, in droves; so much so that native Emiratis make up only about 15 per cent of the total population. Through a massive public relations, advertising and marketing drive, Dubai created its international image, as a place that strove for nothing less than the best: the world's tallest building, the world's longest artificial coastline, the world's largest shopping mall, the world's largest airport. Laying down massive prize money as bait, it lured, and indeed continues to lure, the world's sporting giants to come for horse races, tennis championships and golf tournaments. Celebrities involved were given free suites in luxury hotels, and wined and dined in accordance with the well-publicised Arab hospitality ethic. They still are, but on a slightly tighter budget.

So when this 'Neverland on the never-never', as it was famously described, suddenly announced it could not sustain its debts, the international financial community, brainwashed by Dubai's 'economic miracle' mantra, could hardly believe its ears. With only small oil revenues to

Construction has been hit hard by the economic crisis

fall back on, Dubai was much harder hit by the worldwide freeze in credit markets than its oil-rich neighbour Abu Dhabi. Struggling, washed up on its own beaches even, it was forced to beg for assistance from Abu Dhabi, which, after a nail-biting delay to make Dubai sweat a little, gave it a $10 billion handout so that the government-owned flagship investment conglomerate Dubai World could pay its debts. The current ruler, Sheikh Muhammad, was forced to eat humble pie, and the tiny emirate in the sand showed its vulnerable side.

For holidaymakers, none of this is necessarily bad news. Spare capacity in the luxury hotels means that prices have dropped considerably, and bargains can be had. Dubai is only too delighted to see anyone and everyone who will come.

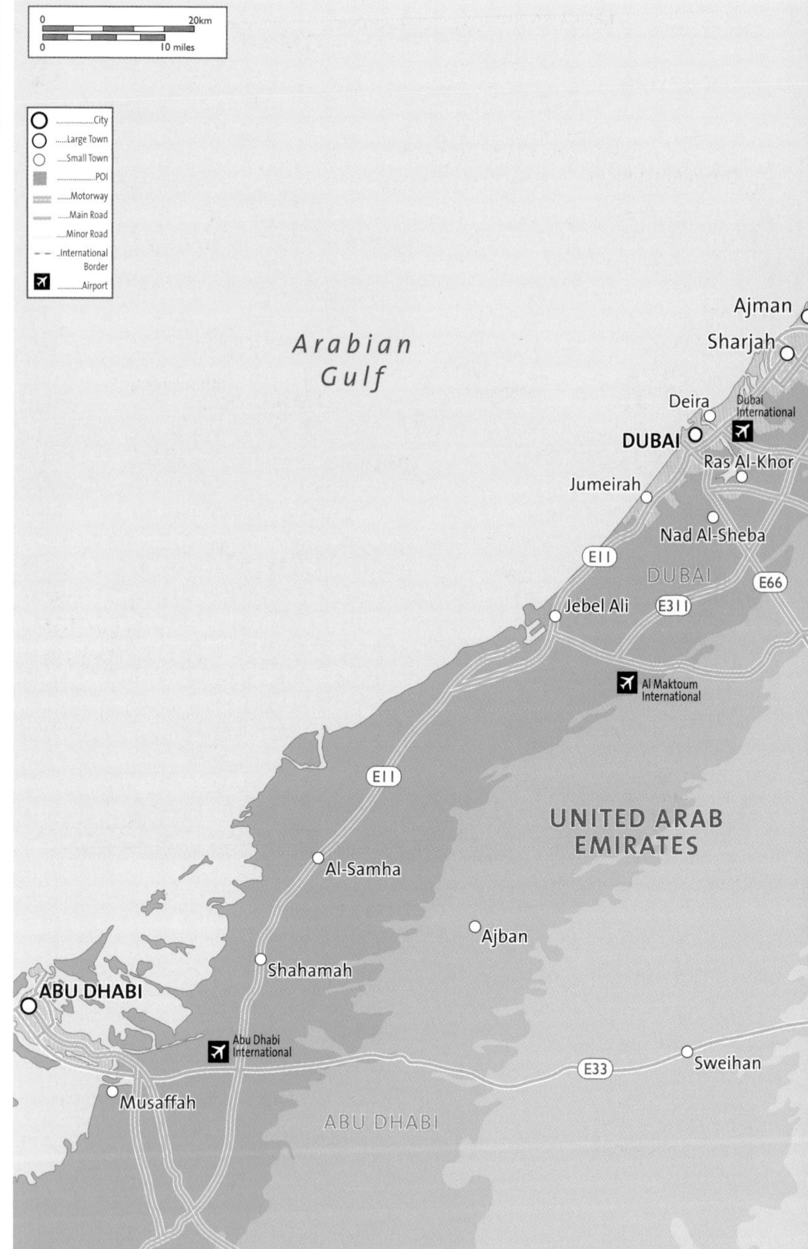
0
20km
0
10 miles
City
Large Town
Small Town
POI
Motorway
Main Road
Minor Road
International Border
Airport
Arabian Gulf
Ajman
Sharjah
Deira
Dubai International
DUBAI
Ras Al-Khor
Jumeirah
Nad Al-Sheba
E11
DUBAI
E66
Jebel Ali
E311
Al Maktoum International
E11
UNITED ARAB EMIRATES
Al-Samha
Ajban
Shahamah
ABU DHABI
Abu Dhabi International
E33
Sweihan
Musaffah
ABU DHABI

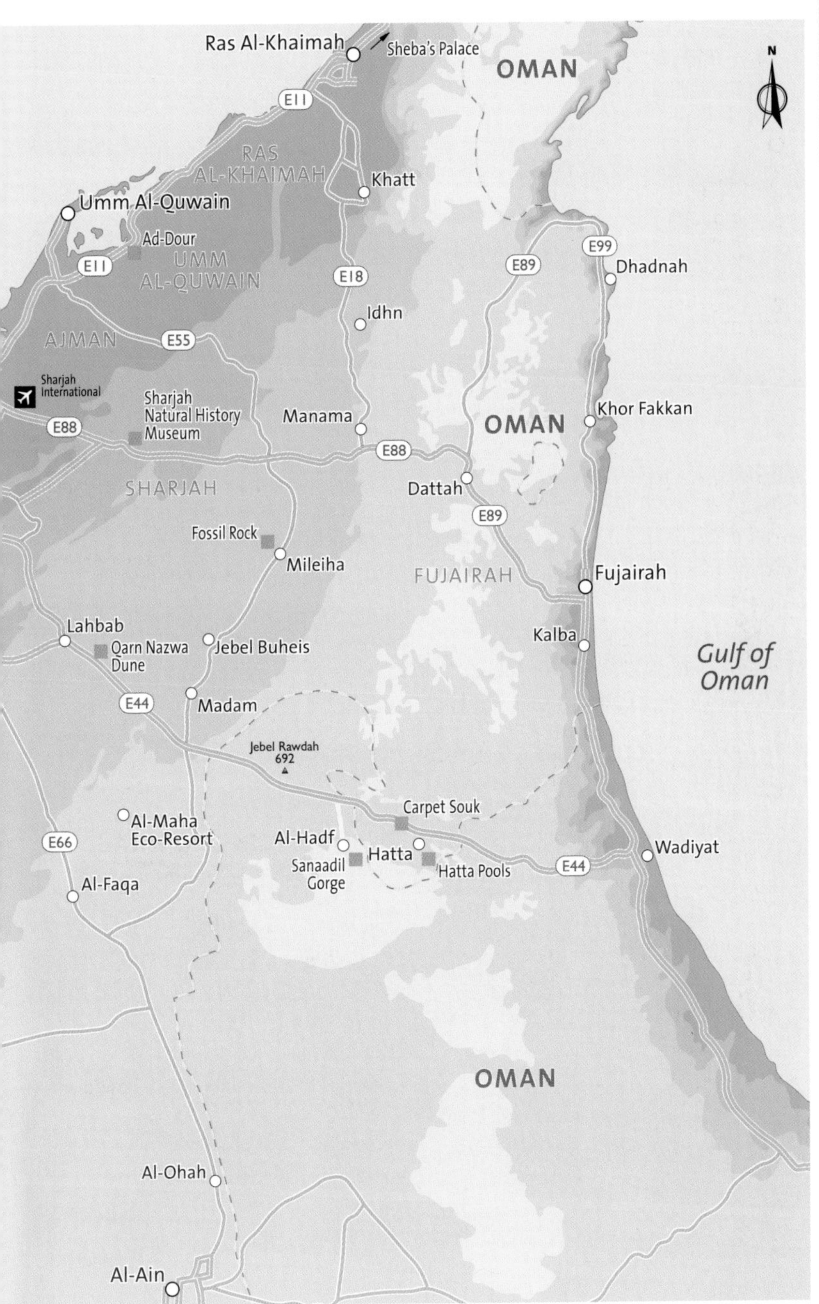
Ras Al-Khaimah
Sheba's Palace
OMAN
N
E11
RAS
AL-KHAIMAH
Khatt
Umm Al-Quwain
Ad-Dour
UMM
AL-QUWAIN
E11
E18
E89
E99
Dhadnah
Idhn
AJMAN
E55
Sharjah
International
Sharjah
Natural History
Museum
E88
Manama
OMAN
Khor Fakkan
E88
Dattah
SHARJAH
E89
Fossil Rock
Mileiha
FUJAIRAH
Fujairah
Lahbab
Qarn Nazwa
Dune
Jebel Buheis
Kalba
Gulf of
Oman
E44
Madam
Jebel Rawdah
692
Carpet Souk
Al-Maha
Eco-Resort
Al-Hadf
Hatta
Wadiyat
E66
Sanaadil
Gorge
Hatta Pools
E44
Al-Faqa
OMAN
Al-Ohah
Al-Ain

The land

It would be a mistake to imagine that Dubai consists purely of a coastline with a flat desert hinterland. Inland, the remarkable geology of the area has created some surprisingly beautiful and impressive mountains in which there are hidden wadis (river valleys), some seasonal, some permanent.

Geology

Some 70–90 million years ago, just before the time the dinosaurs became extinct, volcanic eruptions drove the ocean floor upwards to form the Hajar mountains that straddle the United Arab Emirates and Oman. Geologists get extremely excited about this, for it means that this is one of the very few places in the world where you can study the ocean crust easily on land. Many marine fossils can be found a long way inland, as in Fossil Valley near Al-Ain, where the natural basin collected the skeletons of millions of tiny sea creatures.

Dubai's subtropical gardens require massive amounts of irrigation

The massive Jebel Hafeet Rock at Al-Ain was formed 30–50 million years ago, and its distinctive ridge, known to geologists as an anticline, has drawn much interest because this formation is often associated with oil deposits. The Musandam group of rocks range from 97–200 million years in age and are limestone formations that evolved more gently and gradually than the harder volcanic mountains. The valley that divides the Hajar range from the Musandam range is called the Dibba Fault. At that time, the climate was a great deal wetter, and huge rivers cut out the deep wadis and canyons, such as Siji and Hatta, that you can see today.

Desert

The dunes that are blown southeastwards by the prevailing northwesterly winds range in colour from white and cream to deep red-brown. The desert between Abu Dhabi and Dubai is thoroughly unprepossessing, a drab neutral colour with grey-green camel scrub criss-crossed with vehicle tracks. Yet as you proceed inland it improves, becoming golden and warmer, and at sunset it is a fine deep red that is particularly magnificent. The redness is explained by the presence of iron oxide, a feature of the arid climate. At the end of the last ice age some 15,000 years ago, most of what is now desert was grassland. As a result of huge geological changes that have occurred in the area, archaeologists have discovered ancient sites which a mere 3,000 years ago lay on the seashore, but are now 16km (10 miles) inland.

Sandy terrain suits some

Climate

For six months of the year, mid-April to mid-October, the climate in Dubai is 'bloody awful', as Sir Hugh Bowstead, Britain's first political agent, described it in 1961. Average shade temperatures range from 35–41°C (95–106°F) with an average 97 per cent humidity or total saturation on the coast. Even sea temperatures in summer reach 35–40°C (95–104°F), dropping to around 22°C (72°F) by the end of December. From mid-October to mid-April, however, the climate can be delightful, with clear warm days and fresh starry nights, and only occasional rainfall. Average temperatures range from 15–25°C (59–77°F) and the winter humidity of 78 per cent compares favourably with London's 83 per cent. An extra layer of clothing is needed after dark as the temperature drops very rapidly.

History

3000 BC Umm Al-Nar tombs and settlements built throughout the United Arab Emirates, contemporaneous with Mesopotamian culture. Links with Mesopotamia through copper trading.

1000 BC Iron Age villages and tombs constructed throughout the United Arab Emirates.

326 BC Alexander the Great conquers all lands from Asia Minor (now Turkey) east to the Oxus. Greek culture spreads and Hellenistic cities flourish in the United Arab Emirates.

AD 635 Battle of Dibba marks the completion of the Islamic conversion of Arabia.

7th–17th centuries Julfar, Ras Al-Khaimah, is the major port of the United Arab Emirates, trading with countries as far away as China.

16th–17th centuries Portuguese domination of the region, but there is no religious or cultural legacy. The Portuguese are forced out by the British and Dutch arriving from the sea.

18th–19th centuries The area is dubbed the 'Pirate Coast' by Britain.

1820 The General Treaty of Peace is signed with the British. Henceforth, the area is called Trucial States or Trucial Coast.

1892 An agreement is signed with the Trucial sheikhs not to have any resident agent other than the British.

1922 The sheikhs undertake not to give concessions for oil prospecting except with the approval of the British government.

1930s & 1940s The British draw up boundaries between the different emirates.

1939 The first oil concession is signed by Sheikh Shakhbut.

FORMATION OF THE UNITED ARAB EMIRATES

The impetus to form the federation of the United Arab Emirates in 1971 was the announcement by Britain of its withdrawal from the region as a result of spending cuts under a Labour government. This left a security vacuum that the Gulf countries were very concerned about. Abu Dhabi and Dubai were the driving forces behind the move.

1945–8 War between Dubai and Abu Dhabi over territorial claims. Dubai loses land.

1950 Oil is discovered.

1951 Trucial Oman Scouts are established to maintain order and peace.

1962 First oil exports.

1968 Britain withdraws from the Gulf as part of worldwide cutbacks.

1971 The United Arab Emirates is formed. It creates its own set of laws modelled on those of Egypt, Sudan and Jordan, where French and British law had already been assimilated with the principles of *Shari'a* law (*see p15*).

1979 Sheikh Zayed, ruler of Abu Dhabi and president of the UAE, imposes the centralisation of the welfare state, police, legal system and telecommunications network.

1990 Sheikh Maktoum becomes ruler of Dubai and UAE vice-president.

1991 The United Arab Emirates sends troops to join the allies against Iraq in the first Gulf War.

Futuristic cityscapes are the norm in Dubai

2006 Sheikh Maktoum dies and is succeeded by his brother Sheikh Muhammad.
Weekend changes from Thursday/Friday to Friday/Saturday to improve business contact with the West, and labourers are allowed to form trade unions.
First national elections with partly elected advisory body.

2007 Dubai and Qatar become two of the biggest shareholders in the London Stock Exchange.

2008 The UAE cancels entire debt owed by Iraq, almost $7bn.

2009–11 Dubai is hit by the global financial crisis; many construction projects are suspended. Dubai World is bailed out by $10 billion handout from Abu Dhabi.

Dubai in a different light

Above and beyond all its economic and financial woes, Dubai's image on other fronts has also taken a bit of a battering in recent years. The world's media regularly uncovers stories which show a side of Dubai it does not choose to advertise; holidaymakers may be interested to know a little about such matters, to ensure they do not get into trouble during visits to the emirate. A cautionary note: statistics show Britons are more likely to be arrested in the UAE than in any other country with a large British expatriate community, except Thailand.

Dubai law

Visitors to Dubai, especially long-term visitors, should be aware of certain facts about Dubai law. The face presented by the PR and marketing agencies may lull you into a false sense of security that Dubai is some kind of liberal society based on democratic principles. In practice it is more like a medieval dictatorship, as some British expatriates have found out to their cost, with extremely harsh laws and penalties on drugs, alcohol, sex, fraud and bankruptcy. For example, there is zero tolerance of drink-driving, and offenders lose their licence, are put in prison and have their heads shaved. You also have to be over 21 to drink alcohol.

There is a strict ban on sex outside marriage, and unmarried couples risk prosecution, imprisonment or deportation. Even cohabitation in hotels is illegal, as is adultery and homosexuality. Public displays of affection between the sexes, such as kissing, for instance, can result in arrest and a jail sentence, as recent well-publicised cases prove. People who go bankrupt are put in prison and forbidden to leave the country till any outstanding debts are paid. Their bank accounts are frozen and their credit cards blocked. There is no bail, even for trivial offences such as non-payment of hotel bills.

Getting out

When many construction projects ground to a halt in 2009, suspended or abandoned due to the credit crunch, many expats found themselves without work. Some tried to leave but found they could not, as they had debts in the country, which prevented them leaving. In the frantic scramble to get out of the country,

Immigrant labourers arrive for work on a construction project

some simply abandoned their cars at the airport and got on the first available plane, desperate to escape before their details could be put onto the passport officials' computers.

Others did not have that option, especially the immigrant workers, mainly Indians, Pakistanis and Filipinos, whose passports are taken by their employers when they first arrive in the country, even though this is illegal under Dubai law. These people do the actual work in Dubai, constructing the buildings or working as household servants. Most are lured by promises of high salaries and good working conditions, so they leave their expectant families behind, often even selling land to raise the price for the airfare. On arrival their wages often turn out to be much lower and their living conditions substandard, with ten or more to a dormitory and poor sanitation. Most visits to Dubai are of course trouble-free, but it is as well to know the rules.

Politics

The United Arab Emirates Federation was formed in 1971 out of seven autonomous emirates, namely Abu Dhabi, Dubai, Sharjah, Ras Al-Khaimah, Fujairah, Umm Al-Quwain and Ajman. The total population of the UAE is currently about 4.7 million, of which some 85 per cent is expatriate. In Dubai, foreigners outnumber natives by about six to one.

The United Arab Emirates system of government is enshrined in the constitution of the Federal Supreme Council, consisting of the rulers of the seven emirates, a president (always the ruler of Abu Dhabi), a vice-president (always the ruler of Dubai), a Council of Ministers and a Federal Assembly drawn from all the emirates. Since summer 2006, half of the 40-strong Federal Assembly has been elected, while the other half is still appointed. The Assembly only has a consultative role.

Dubai's policy is to build the biggest and best

There are no political parties and there is no universal suffrage, yet with free health care and education, a booming economy and political stability, few have reason to complain. Democracy is not yet a high priority for Dubai's young, who are the best-educated and most-travelled Arabs in the region.

Abu Dhabi can boast around 10 per cent of the world's proven oil reserves and 5 per cent of the world's gas. With the proceeds, it has developed an impressive investment portfolio financed from oil revenue. Dubai has far more limited oil reserves and has, therefore, done things differently. It has diversified into other fields and built on its reputation as a regional entrepôt, making its mark as a top destination for tourists and businesspeople alike, investing millions

HUMAN RIGHTS

The human rights record of the United Arab Emirates is average for this part of the world, with Islamic *Shari'a* law not applied comprehensively. Death sentences and amputations are rarely carried out. A wide range of religions is permitted and a fairly tolerant attitude is taken to Westerners and their alcohol consumption, except in Sharjah, which remains 'dry'. Women are not discriminated against in law, but only a handful play a role in political and commercial decision-making. The inhuman treatment and living conditions endured by some Indian construction workers has recently come under scrutiny from human rights organisations.

in leisure and sporting infrastructures. The other northern emirates, however, fare less well and are dependent on Abu Dhabi and handouts from the federal government.

Dubai, and the United Arab Emirates in general, has succeeded in projecting a carefully controlled image of excellent security and political stability, though the risk of terrorist activity is perceived by the FCO as similar here to most other Arab countries. Although it is not in evidence on the streets, there is in practice a disciplined and effective police and internal security apparatus that usually ensures that any incident is nipped in the bud. The United Arab Emirates strongly condemned the 9/11 World Trade Center terrorist attacks in the USA in 2001, and also sided with the Western allies in the first and second Gulf wars. Relations with Iran have been soured by the dispute over the sovereignty of the islands of Abu Musa, and the Greater and Lesser Tunb in the Gulf. Land border disputes between the emirates used to erupt periodically until as late as 1979, but the arrival of prospecting oil companies meant that formal boundaries had to be agreed.

Depiction of Sheikh Zayed, founder of the United Arab Emirates

Culture

The transition, in the space of some 35 years, from a traditional society to sudden affluence and urbanisation has created demographic problems that are the unavoidable consequence of the sheer pace of development. Those elements of the national population that benefited from the oil wealth have inevitably contributed to a high-consuming society, dependent on a large expatriate workforce, and thereby creating a social and gender imbalance.

Early days

In the 18th and 19th centuries, the population of all seven emirates is thought never to have exceeded 100,000, scattered in small villages mainly on the coast, eking out a subsistence living. These coastal settlements relied almost entirely on the sea for their livelihood, with men working as fishermen, pearl divers or boat builders. Inland life could only be supported in a few desert oases with very limited agriculture. The main staples were dates from the palm trees,

Dubai aims for cultural harmony

camel's milk and fish. Other basic necessities, such as rice and cloth, were bought with pearls traded through the Iranian ports like Bandar Abbas and Lingah, just on the other side of the Gulf. Remarkably little has been documented of everyday life in the emirates pre-oil, although it is important to remember that the Arabian Peninsula had a strong oral tradition, with stories passed by word of mouth from one generation to the next.

Futuristic buildings adorned with traditional images

Changing lifestyles

The discovery of oil has, of course, put paid to these old ways of life, but even though the wealth is now mind-boggling, a sense of the past is still considered important and is being kept alive. Sheikh Zayed of Abu Dhabi reputedly said: 'A nation without a past has neither a present nor a future.' Yet Arab traditions and culture are increasingly exposed to external sources such as satellite television, videos, electronic games, pop music and fashions. The more these come to dominate, the more the local identity is diluted and weakened. One hundred and fifty nationalities now live and work in Dubai. Nationals also employ large numbers of domestic staff from Sri Lanka and the Indian subcontinent, who have come with their own customs and values. Mixed marriages occur between nationals and foreigners, nearly half of which end in divorce.

The solution that the government is working towards is to reduce the demographic imbalance by adopting gradual nationalisation through the employment of qualified local people, and producing a national population that gradually consumes less and contributes more to the country's development.

EDUCATION

Adult literacy is now at 90 per cent, and most of the illiterate are over 40. The most astonishing strides have been achieved by native women, whose literacy rate grew from 0 per cent in 1960 to 33 per cent in 1980 and 90 per cent in 2007. In United Arab Emirates' universities, 65 per cent of students are now women, about half of whom move into the workplace; the other half are often prevented by husbands or parents. They strive to achieve excellence and have ambitions to improve their lot, while their brothers often drop out of studying, having lost their drive and work ethic in a society where so much is already handed out on a plate to men.

Festivals and events

Dubai, ever true to its business ethos, has perfected the art of the festival as a commercial vehicle, creating demand where there was none before. No place on earth so tiny organises so many festivals and events; instead of the 'Build it and they will come' motto, it could be 'Arrange it and they will come'. The best websites to keep abreast of what's on are www.dubaicityguide.com *and* www.godubai.com

Religious festivals

As a Muslim country, Dubai has two major religious festivals (in Arabic, *eids*) a year. The dates are governed by the lunar Islamic calendar which is 11 days shorter than the Western Gregorian calendar. The smaller *eid*, Eid Al-Fitr (Feast of the Breaking of the Fast), can be regarded as the equivalent of the West's Easter, and follows the end of the month of fasting, Ramadan. It is usually a public holiday of three days. The major *eid*, Eid Al-Adha (Feast of the Sacrifice), can be seen as the equivalent of the West's Christmas, and commemorates the willingness of Abraham to sacrifice his son Isaac, and is generally a public holiday of four days. During the *eids*, there used to be a tradition of giving to the needy, but in today's consumer society the emphasis seems to have shifted to spending money on oneself and buying new clothes.

RAMADAN

This 30-day-long period of abstinence from bodily pleasures is one of the five pillars of Islam, and the Koran stipulates that during daylight hours no Muslim can eat, drink, smoke or have sexual intercourse. Working hours are reduced during Ramadan and tempers can get frayed, especially in the first few days when the body is adjusting to the fast. The self-denial is regarded as purification of the soul, enhancing closeness to God. In practice, perversely, more food is consumed during Ramadan than at any other time of the year. The big hotels vie with one another to lay on the most lavish buffets, often set up in special Ramadan tents in the gardens. Most hotel restaurants stay open throughout the day, simply adding special *iftar* (fast-breaking) menus for the sundown feast. The exact timing, to the minute, when the fast may be broken is listed every day in the papers. Eating then continues apace until the small hours.

Local festivals and major sporting events

Dubai has a very active social calendar with many international sporting events. The biggest of these is the Dubai World Cup, the world's richest horse race (*see pp76–7*). As well as the sporting events, where the prize money attracts the world's top players, Dubai hosts shopping and entertainment festivals, and music and cultural programmes, held at various indoor and outdoor venues all year round. The biggest home-grown bonanza is the Dubai Shopping Festival (*see pp20–21*).

January
Dubai International Sailing Week Regatta, Dubai Marathon, Dubai Shopping Festival, Emirates Cup Traditional Dhow Sailing Race

February
Dubai International Jazz Festival, Dubai Tennis Championships, Dubai Terry Fox Run, International Festival of Literature

Ramadan is also celebrated in the shopping malls

March
Dubai Desert Golf Classic, Dubai International Kite Surfing Challenge, Dubai World Cup

April
International Jewellery Exhibition

May
Dubai Worldwide Property Show, Traditional Dhow Racing at Al-Mina Al-Seyahi

June
Dubai Summer Surprises, United Arab Emirates National Sailing Championship

July
Dubai Summer Surprises

August
Dubai Summer Surprises

September
Dubai the City that Cares Festival

October
Gulf IT Exhibition (GITEX), United Arab Emirates Desert Challenge

November
Dubai Traditional Dhow Sailing Race, Horse-racing season

December
Dubai Air Show, Dubai Grand Prix, National Day Celebrations, Rugby Sevens

Dubai Shopping Festival

Dubai has found its month-long Shopping Festival, inaugurated in 1996, to be so lucrative that it has now become a regular fixture. Even the build-up to the annual festival is on an impressive scale. Projects to do with retailing or encouraging people to spend money pull out all the stops to ensure that their completion coincides with the start of the Shopping Festival. Hence Dubai's Heritage Village on the Creek was completed from scratch in a remarkable six months to make sure it was ready in time for the start of the 1997 festival, as was Umm Suqeim's new Spinneys Centre.

Price reductions

All the major shopping malls reduce prices, although resident sceptics say that prices are artificially inflated before the festival so that they can appear to be reduced when it begins. The big malls like Mall of the Emirates, Ibn Battuta Mall, Deira City Centre and BurJuman offer spectacular prizes such as Lexus or Grand Nissan cars in lottery-style draws that can be entered by anyone spending over a certain amount, usually Dh100. The prize draws take place every evening in the various malls at around 9pm, when the hopefuls congregate in droves.

Expensive cars are raffled off in the malls during the Shopping Festival

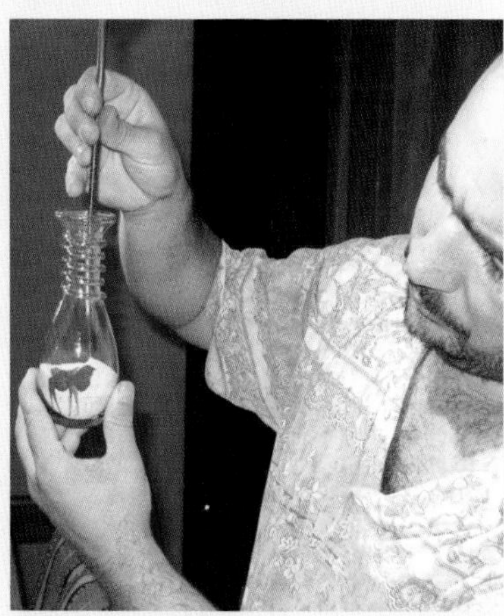

A craftsman at work making sand souvenirs

Hot-air balloons, fireworks, lasers, carnivals, funfairs and even a circus take place daily, and the *Gulf News* has a special supplement detailing the events of the day, such as bungee-jumping at the Creek or the International Gold Conference.

Themed shopping

Popular shopping themes are recreations of Arab souks (traditional markets with stalls) from all over the Arab world such as Cairo's Khan Al-Khalili and the souks of Morocco, Syria and Yemen.

At the Carpet Oasis, over 150,000 carpets are usually for sale at heavily discounted prices, and at the Global Village, which has now been moved from its former Creekside location to out beyond the Sheikh Zayed highway, souvenirs are for sale from every corner of the globe in buildings that represent the culture of the relevant country such as pagodas, Mogul palaces or Pharaonic temples (*www.globalvillage.ae*). Running alongside the Shopping Festival, other events are scheduled to complement it, such as the Sports Festival, Food Festival and Fashion Festival, as well as a smattering of cultural and folkloric performances.

Many of the special features designed for the festival, like the Rigga Street pavement cafés and pedestrian zone, become permanent fixtures afterwards. The number of visitors arriving for the festival, mainly from the subcontinent and the rest of the Arab world, usually exceeds the total United Arab Emirates population of 3.5 million. The neighbouring emirates of Abu Dhabi and Sharjah are said to feel the pinch during the festival, as Dubai creams off all the business for itself, with little or no spillover for them.

Terrific publicity is bought in for the event, with Western TV teams, for example, flown in on full expenses to cover the festival. Hotels record full capacity and some offer up to 40 per cent discounts as incentives. The festival even has its own website (*www.dubaishoppingfestival.com*).

Highlights

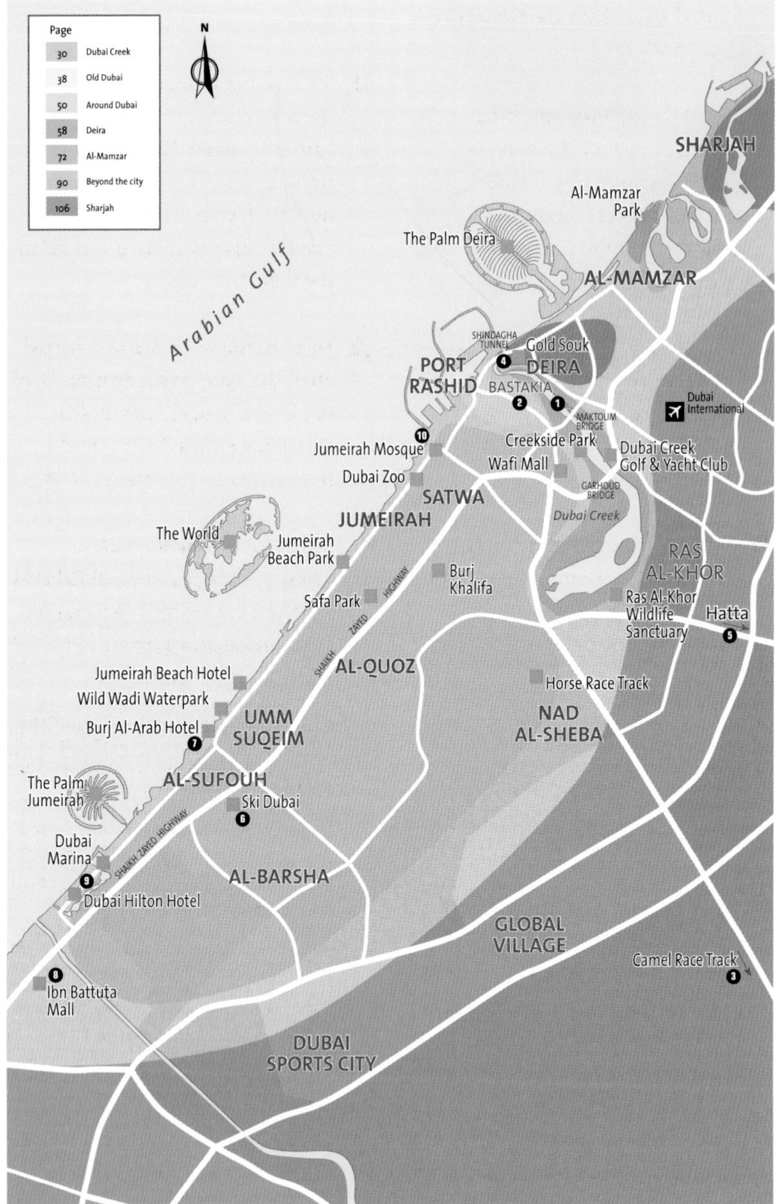
Page
30 Dubai Creek
38 Old Dubai
50 Around Dubai
58 Deira
72 Al-Mamzar
90 Beyond the city
106 Sharjah
N
Arabian Gulf
SHARJAH
Al-Mamzar Park
The Palm Deira
AL-MAMZAR
SHINDAGHA TUNNEL
Gold Souk
DEIRA
PORT RASHID
BASTAKIA
MAKTOUM BRIDGE
Dubai International
Jumeirah Mosque
Creekside Park
Dubai Creek Golf & Yacht Club
Wafi Mall
Dubai Zoo
GARHOUD BRIDGE
SATWA
Dubai Creek
JUMEIRAH
The World
Jumeirah Beach Park
RAS AL-KHOR
Burj Khalifa
SHAIKH ZAYED HIGHWAY
Safa Park
Ras Al-Khor Wildlife Sanctuary
Hatta
AL-QUOZ
Jumeirah Beach Hotel
Horse Race Track
Wild Wadi Waterpark
UMM SUQEIM
NAD AL-SHEBA
Burj Al-Arab Hotel
The Palm Jumeirah
AL-SUFOUH
Ski Dubai
Dubai Marina
AL-BARSHA
Dubai Hilton Hotel
GLOBAL VILLAGE
Camel Race Track
Ibn Battuta Mall
DUBAI SPORTS CITY

❶ Enjoy a relaxing evening cruise in a luxurious traditional dhow, with dinner along the Dubai Creek (*see pp30–31*).

❷ Stroll through the renovated Bastakia quarter, the only remaining part of old Dubai, with its *barjeel* (wind towers) and typical Arab courtyard houses (*see pp36–7*).

❸ Get up early to watch the desert camel racing, with literally hundreds of colourfully garbed camels set against the futuristic Dubai skyline (*see pp98–9*).

❹ Immerse yourself in the massive Gold Souk of Deira, where prices are among the cheapest in the world (*see pp62–3*).

❺ Rent a four-wheel-drive vehicle, take a picnic and drive an hour out of the city to explore the striking volcanic mountains and wadis around Hatta (*see pp94–5*).

❻ Experiment on the ski slopes of Ski Dubai within the Mall of the Emirates at temperatures of –5°C (23°F), then pop to the next-door café for an après-ski drink in front of the log fire (*see p85*).

❼ Take afternoon tea or sip exotic cocktails, drinking in the ambience and the view from the top-floor Sky View Bar of the iconic 'seven-star' Burj Al-Arab Hotel (*see pp79, 82–3*).

❽ Spend an afternoon shopping in the magnificent Ibn Battuta Mall, and learn about Arabic culture from the superbly designed panels depicting Arab inventors, doctors and scientists that are displayed in the walkways (*see p52*).

❾ Swim in the warm sea and sprawl afterwards on the sandy beaches of one of the many luxury hotels, sustaining yourself with snacks from the beach bar (*see pp80–81*).

❿ Take a tour of the Jumeirah Mosque, built in medieval Fatimid style and one of the few mosques non-Muslims are permitted to enter in Dubai (*see p45*).

The beautifully designed interior of the Ibn Battuta Mall

Suggested itineraries

Dubai is becoming popular even for long weekend breaks, despite its distance from Europe. However, ideally at least a week should be allowed to enjoy the place properly and to get a chance to relax as well.

Half-day excursions out of Dubai

Ajman fort/museum.
Hatta road, good for desert driving practice and for sand-skiing.
Jebel Buheis for scenery and archaeology.
Jebel Maleihah – also for scenery and archaeology.
Qarn Nazwa Dune (picnic lunch) – half an hour's drive from Dubai city on the way to Sharjah's museums.
Sharjah's old restored souks (markets).

Full-day excursions from Dubai

Dubai is the most centrally located of the emirates and has the best road connections. If you are prepared to make early starts and do not mind drives of up to two hours each way, the following destinations make good outings from Dubai city:

- Al-Ain (zoo and tombs), Jebel Hafeet, Al-Ain fort (picnic lunch) – 90 minutes' drive from the city.
- Ad-Dour, Tell Abraq, archaeology and scenery (picnic lunch) – 90 minutes' drive from the city.
- Al-Hadf/Sanaadil Gorge (picnic lunch) – one hour's drive from the city.
- Hatta, Heritage Village, pools and tombs (picnic lunch or eat at Hatta Fort Hotel) – one hour's drive from the city.
- Bithnah fort and Wadi Hayl (picnic lunch) – 90 minutes' drive from the city.
- Fujairah fort and museum (picnic lunch or eat at a hotel) – two hours' drive from the city.

Al-Ain fort was built in 1910 for the ruling family

Relax on one of Dubai's sandy beaches for one day over a long weekend

- Ras Al-Khaimah fort/museum (picnic lunch or eat at a hotel) – two hours' drive from the city.
- Sheba's Palace and Shimmel Necropolis, Ras Al-Khaimah (picnic lunch), archaeology and scenery – two hours' drive from the city.
- Umm Al-Quwain fort/museum, Aquarium (picnic lunch) – 90 minutes' drive from the city.

Long weekend

Day 1 Fly into Dubai.
Day 2 Visit Old Dubai's Bastakia quarter and Dubai Museum, explore the Creek by *abra* (crossing boat) and see Deira's Gold Souk.
Day 3 Take a day trip to the mountain enclave of Hatta, stopping at the dunes en route.
Day 4 Spend a day resting on the beach and doing a bit of mall shopping.
Day 5 Return flight.

One week

With one full week at your disposal, a good balance would be two days spent exploring the sights of Dubai city, two days shopping in the various malls (especially the Mall of the Emirates and the Ibn Battuta Mall) and the Gold Souk, one day on an excursion out of the city, say to Hatta, and two days lounging on the hotel beach and by the pool.

Two weeks

An additional week will allow you to do the one-week itinerary (*see above*), and you can add a few more excursions to the other emirates, all of which are described in this guide (*see pp100–119*). Alternatively, if you don't mind the extra driving, you could even cross the border into Oman, getting a visa on the spot.

CAR HIRE

Car hire in Dubai is extremely cheap; unlimited mileage costs from £85 a week with reputable companies like Thrifty, and the road network is excellent. Driving on the city's eight-lane Sheikh Zayed Highway requires care, but the only other problem can be maintaining your sense of direction at the complex flyover junctions that may throw you off course. To compensate, signposting is excellent on the whole.

Dubai city

Dubai is the largest city in the UAE, bigger than the capital, Abu Dhabi city. Its name, perhaps fittingly, comes from a local locust, daba, *which consumes anything before it. Dubai post credit-crunch is intent on regaining its credibility on the world stage. Only one of the much-heralded Palm Islands has been completed, and The World, a mega-ambitious scheme of islands representing all the countries of the globe is, in the words of its lawyer, 'in a coma', gradually sinking back into the sea.*

ENVIRONMENTAL IMPACT

Dubai used to boast about its massive schemes to conquer the environment, making the desert bloom into lush green golf courses, creating giant freezers to fashion indoor ski slopes and beaches with air-conditioning built in under the sand. Now this boast rings more than a little hollow, as statistics reveal that each Dubai resident has the biggest carbon footprint of any human being in the world – double that of an

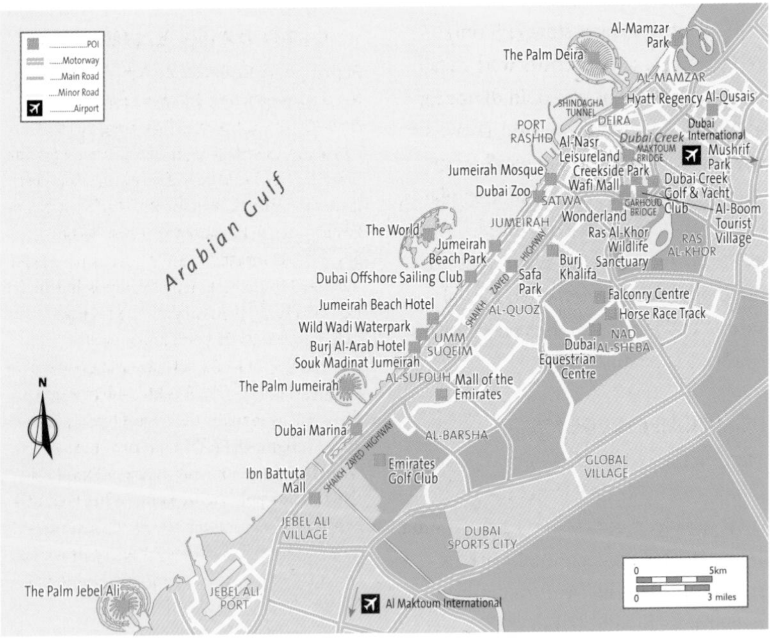

Homes on the 'fronds' of the Palm, Jumeirah

American. Tiger Woods' proposed golf course, for example, currently on hold awaiting finance, would need four million gallons of water a day to keep it green, otherwise it would wither in a matter of days. In fact all of Dubai would wither, as the capacity for water storage is only about a week, so if revenues were to fail totally, the entire place would disappear into the sand within a month. There is no natural local water supply, so all water currently comes from desalination plants, the production of which is more expensive than the equivalent in petrol – not to mention the vast quantities of carbon emissions the desalination plants belch into the atmosphere.

POLITICAL FREEDOMS

Despite the veneer of a liberal society, Dubai (and the UAE generally) exercises strict censorship of the media. Internet sites are regulated, with no sites permitted that feature dating networks, gays and lesbians, pornography, or any sites originating from Israel. Ironically, in spite of these restrictions, Dubai is well known as the 'gay capital' of the Gulf, and also has its fair share of prostitutes.

O, TO BE AN EMIRATI...

Emiratis have total security. Most work for the government and are therefore cushioned from the credit crunch. They are given free education to PhD level, a free house on getting married, free healthcare, free phone calls, and no taxes to pay; Dubai for them is like a 'Santa Claus state'. To be sacked you have to be beyond incompetence, and the laws have been tightened to make it virtually impossible to get rid of an Emirati employee. The average income is $120,000 per annum. Not surprisingly, most do not have much by way of complaints. They like Sheikh Muhammad on the whole, seeing him as a great leader. They are not frightened of him as some kind of despot, and are not really bothered much by their lack of political freedom. What about the expats, they are sometimes asked, don't they annoy you? 'Yes,' they reply, 'the expats are an eyesore, but they are the price we had to pay for this development.'

BUR DUBAI SIDE OF THE CREEK

The western side of Dubai's Creek is known locally as Bur Dubai, meaning 'Port Dubai'. Throughout its history, Dubai's raison d'être has been to trade, using its sheltered creek for safe harbourage between Iran, India and Pakistan to the east, and central Arabia and Africa to the west. It began as a small trading port in the 18th century. In 1822, the commander of the British ship *Discovery* described it: 'The town is an assemblage of mud hovels surrounded by a low mud wall.'

At that time, there were about 1,000–1,200 inhabitants, with 150 Nubian soldiers to guard the town. Dubai was supported by pearling, sending 90 ships to pearl each season. Its small population was then given a boost by the arrival in 1833 of 800 or more Bedouin who left their oases of Liwa and Al-Ain to settle in Dubai and base their livelihoods on the sea, with fishing, pearling and trade. They belonged to the Beni Yas tribe, as did the Abu Dhabi Bedouin, and were known as the Al-Bu Flasah. Up until that point, Dubai had been a dependency of Abu Dhabi, but the new Dubai leader Maktoum Bin Butti ruled until 1852, and thereby established the separate Maktoum Dynasty that still rules Dubai today. The Al-Bu Flasah settled in the area now called Shindagha, around the Sheikh Saeed House.

The lights of Dubai reflect off the Creek at night

Ferries shuttle passengers across the Creek

Dubai's population of merchants was given a further boost when in 1902 all ports on the Iranian coast put up their customs dues dramatically for imports and exports. A large group of Iranian merchants from Lingah, the dominant Persian port of the time, moved to Dubai, which was directly opposite. Indian merchants had also come across, attracted by the flourishing trade, to set up shops in the souk (market), so that even by the 1930s a quarter of the population of Dubai was of foreign origin, with Iranians the dominant minority.

In Dubai, anything goes if it makes money. Its policy throughout its recent history has been to maximise all possible means for economic expansion. Many likened it to a boom town in the Wild West, and the raw commercialism of the place was a little shocking to new arrivals. While weathering the financial crisis, though, its horns have been withdrawn for the moment.

THE SAFETY OF THE UNDESIRED

A 20th-century historian, Stephen Longrigg, gave his explanation of why this part of the world escaped colonialism as follows: 'They have enjoyed the safety of the undesired, and have lived lives to which a hundred generations have specialised them, in conditions barely tolerable to others.'

Recent history could hardly be more different, with Dubai seeking to attract foreigners to invest and make money.

Boat trip: Dubai Creek

Dubai city's only geographical feature is the Creek, which is the reason for its development as a successful trading port with Iran and India. The boat trip takes one to two hours, over a distance of 8km (5 miles).

1 Bastakia quarter

The best place to pick up an *abra*, the little motorised boats with awnings that cross between the two sides of the Creek, is probably near the Bastakia quarter. There are a number of individual boats for hire and the larger plusher traditional boats for evening dinner cruises are moored here. Avoid the actual *abra* crossing points unless all you want to do is make the crossing over to the Deira (eastern) side, to visit the Gold Souk, for example. You will have to negotiate your price for hiring the boat, but fares are not usually exorbitant.

2 Wharfage

A boat is definitely the best way to view the extraordinary collection of hundreds of colourful dhows that line the Deira side of the Creek. The dhows'

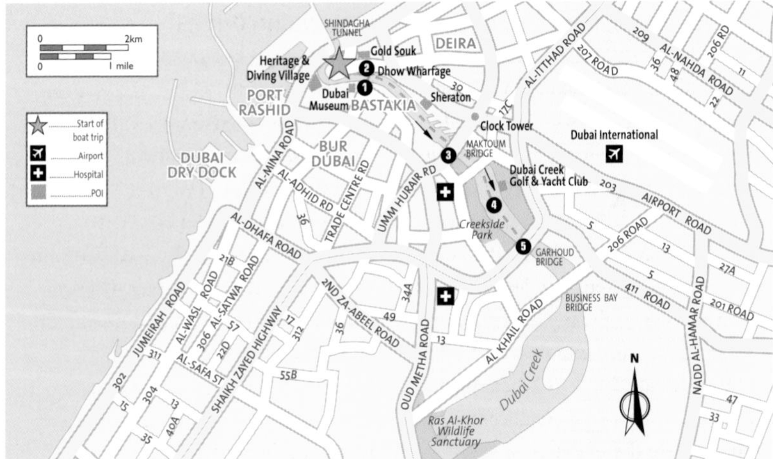

Abras, water taxis, waiting on the Creek

destinations remain Iran and India, but instead of gold from India, today the dhows arrive laden with caviar and carpets from Iran, and return with electrical goods and Levi jeans.

The Indian government has clamped down on smuggling in recent decades, so these days there is more smuggling from Iran. A small but steady trade of smuggled products from endangered animals, like ivory and leopard skin, has also been discovered. The Deira side of the Creek, where the big hotels like the Hyatt Regency, the InterContinental and the Sheraton (*see p161*) stand, has always been the commercial centre of Dubai, where the majority of souks were located, while the fort and the ruler's palace stood on what was, and still is, considered to be the more residential side, known as Bur Dubai. The impressive modern architecture of the hotels and international banks dominates the skyline of the Deira side beyond the dhow wharfage.

3 Maktoum Bridge

This was the first bridge to cross the Creek, built in the 1970s under Sheikh Rashid. There are now several bridges to help ease the congestion, including a temporary floating pontoon between Maktoum and Garhoud bridges.

4 Creekside Park

After the Maktoum Bridge, the Creek widens, with the Creekside Park to the west and the Dubai Creek Golf and Yacht Club, with its unmistakable clubhouse built in the shape of a tent, to the east.

5 Garhoud Bridge

The *abra* will not go beyond the next bridge, Garhoud, although the Creek itself opens considerably and widens. Today it is 12km (7½ miles) long and on average 0.5km (⅓ mile) wide. When it was dredged under the instructions of Sheikh Rashid in the late 1960s, the spoil was used in nearby low-lying areas to create new building land along the Creek shore that had previously flooded at high tide. The sale of this new land greatly offset the dredging costs.

Dubai Museum

Established in the Al-Fahidi ruler's fort by order of Sheikh Rashid in 1971, the museum sits in the busy market area of Bur Dubai near the head of the Creek that it once guarded. These days, the fort's view of the Creek is entirely obliterated by commercial buildings.

The sandy-coloured fort towers are very impressive, and a huge life-size model of a dhow stands beside the museum in an open space, under which you later discover is the modern underground section of the museum, part of the clever and extensive renovation project that was completed in 1995.

As you enter the main gateway, take a moment to examine the splendid teak door and the fine brass door knockers. The courtyard contains some fascinating examples of types of boats used for fishing, and a charming *barasti* (palm frond) hut with a summer room to allow breezes through and a snug winter room within. There is a fine collection of weapons, including shark-fin shields and chain-mail suits. Weapons always held an important place in Dubai, and all men traditionally carried one. In a long room off the courtyard, there is a display of local musical instruments, from a harp, and bagpipes made from goatskin, to a percussion shaker made of goat's hooves.

The museum's one-way system now leads you down the spiral ramp past

Cannons flank the entrance to the Dubai Museum

A traditional dhow outside the Dubai Museum

stuffed seabirds and a flamingo to reach recreations of the Creek as it was before the discovery of oil in the 1950s. A display board claims that the Creek used to go inland as far as Al-Ain, 140km (87 miles) away. A brief film then takes you through a visual kaleidoscope from the 1930s to the present day, and from here you pop through into the reconstruction of the 1960s souk (market), which is startlingly real with sound effects and even smells. Beyond the souk, the reconstruction runs to a Koranic school and a traditional house with a display that explains the children's toys. The stuffed camel in the alleyway is especially fine, and can even be petted and stroked.

From here, the theme progresses to the desert, with camels, oases and dates. The importance of water is explained, and the corridor leads on into a wildlife display area with the desert by night and a Bedouin tent. Next you move on to the sun, moon and astronomy section with stars and wind, which illustrates the ways in which camel caravans and ships used to navigate. After this, you step into the marine gallery, designed as an underwater setting with boats above your head, displaying the fish found in local waters.

The final section before the bookshop and exit is archaeology, with finds from the Hatta tombs, the burials at Al-Qusais and the Mound of Serpents (*see p66*), as well as the Al-Jumeirah Islamic caravan city.

Al-Fahidi Fort, Bur Dubai. Tel: 353 1862. Open: Sat–Thur 8.30am–8.30pm, Fri 2.30–8.30pm. Admission charge. Parking is difficult at busy shopping times; it is better to visit between 1pm and 4pm when most of the shops shut and the adjacent car park with coin meters may have spaces.

Pearl diving

Before the advent of oil in the 1950s, pearling was the main source of income for the populations living along the coast. Most of the pearl banks in the Arabian Gulf are closer to the Arabian than the Persian coastline, and although their locations had been known for centuries, none was claimed as the property of a particular sheikhdom, and so all were open to any boat from the Arab ports. So skilful were the captains of the pearling boats that they used to find their way to the pearl bank of their choice with no maps or compasses, using only aids like the sun, the stars and the colour and depth of the water. The boats were equipped with sails and oars, and in calm conditions the already exhausted divers had to row from one pearl bank to another. Some captains stayed by a particular pearl bank most of the season, while others liked to move frequently between banks.

The pearling season lasted around 120 days, from early June to late September, but if Ramadan fell during the summer, it was sometimes brought forward by a month, as diving was prohibited during the fast. Slaves formed over 80 per cent of the diving population, which was one major reason why the local sheikhs

A pearling chest with a selection of sieves

Weighing out the pearl catch

were not keen to implement the slave trade agreements signed with the British. If the divers had been given their freedom, the loss to the pearling trade would have been extremely serious. The ownership of house-born slaves was a long-standing tradition, and the master of the household legitimately took his share of the dive.

Only the exceptionally large or perfect pearls were sold individually, and the fortunate diver who found such a pearl would be well recompensed. The remainder were carefully graded using a series of copper sieves with five different-sized holes. Then they were sold in bulk to a middleman, who would frequently come from Dubai. The middleman would sell the pearls on to the Indian pearl merchants who came over, generally from Bombay, for the season. India was the age-old market for pearls, and after they became fashionable in Britain and then in the USA in the 20th century, the result was something of a boom in the pearl market, reaching its peak in 1929. The hierarchy of the pearling industry was so complex that special divers' courts were set up to resolve disputes.

PEARL OYSTERS

There are three types of oyster that produce pearls in the Gulf, and each type has its preferred depth, ranging from the low-tide mark to 36m (118ft), and its preferred conditions of light, currents, type of seabed and feeding matter. The oyster forms the pearl after a tiny particle of grit has penetrated its shell, causing the oyster to secrete layer upon layer of mother-of-pearl (the scientific name is 'nacre' from the Arabic *naqqara* meaning 'small drum') over the particle of grit. The most perfect pearls were generally found at the greatest depths, so captains with good and experienced divers headed for those.

Bastakia

The Bastakia quarter on the Bur Dubai edge of the Creek is Dubai's only remaining district of old housing, complete with picturesque *barjeel* (wind towers). Many houses were knocked down as recently as the 1980s, notably to make way for the ruler's Diwan (administrative) Office on the Creekside, but the Dubai Municipality Historic Buildings Section has now designated the area for conservation and has been gradually restoring all the buildings and converting them into offices for its own headquarters, a tourist and information centre, and the

Wind towers in the Bastakia quarter

Calligraphy House. There are now even a couple of small hotels built in traditional style around the courtyard, and there are restaurants and cafés in the restored old buildings.

The houses here were originally built in 1902 by a group of Iranian merchants. They had left their home town of Lingah on the Iranian coast after high customs duties were introduced there, threatening their livelihoods, and they looked across to the trading haven of Dubai where no taxes were levied at all. Their district was named Bastakia after the Bastakia region in southern Persia, from where many of them originated. They built the region beside the Dubai souk and directly opposite the Deira souk, which was the largest along the Gulf at that time, with about 350 shops. Unlike most Persians who were Shia, these were mainly Sunni and of distant Arab origin. The skills of these merchants played a large role in Dubai's ability to withstand the collapse of the pearling industry in the 1930s by enabling the emirate to develop an entrepôt trade with Persia and India throughout the 1940s and 1950s. Dubai's cosmopolitan links gave it a head start in the late 1960s when oil revenues began to flow in, and the Iranian merchants were rewarded with United Arab Emirates nationality when the United Arab Emirates Federation was set up in 1971.

Traditional restoration work in Bastakia

BARJEEL

Until the beginning of the 20th century, the *barjeel* (wind tower) had not been known, and the local inhabitants had lived in *barasti* (palm frond) huts that allowed the breeze to pass through the walls. The principle of the wind tower is to collect breeze from any direction and funnel it down the chimney to the room below, usually the *majlis* (reception room). In winter, this could make the room draughty, so the base of the tower was generally sealed off with specially cut wooden sections until the heat arrived again. The Persians introduced this architectural feature to Dubai and to all of the United Arab Emirates, and soon even *barasti* huts were constructed with wind towers, as the one in the courtyard of the Dubai Museum demonstrates (*see p32*).

The foundations of the Bastakia houses were made of *sarouj*, a mixture of manure and red clay from Iran dried and baked in a kiln; the houses themselves were made of coral stone cut from the banks of the Creek, limestone slabs, and plaster for the decorative finish. There were some 50 Bastakia houses, each designed around a courtyard for a large extended family.

Walk: Old Dubai

This stroll around what remains of Old Dubai is essentially along the western side of the Creek, Dubai's original raison d'être. You will see an interesting and varied selection of buildings and landmarks that will give you a picture of Dubai's earlier history and traditional life.

Allow half a day (3–4 hours), which includes an hour spent in the museum itself. The total distance is about 3km (1¾ miles).

If you are here in the summer months, make sure you do this walk either early in the morning or after dark, as there is little shade.

1 Bastakia quarter

There are three parking areas around the Bastakia quarter, all just off the Al-Fahidi roundabout, so these are where you should aim for the start of your walk. From here it is easy to visit and stroll around the alleyways of these old houses with their picturesque wind towers (*see pp36–7*). The car parks have meters that take coins. The quarter is developing an appealing arty feel and

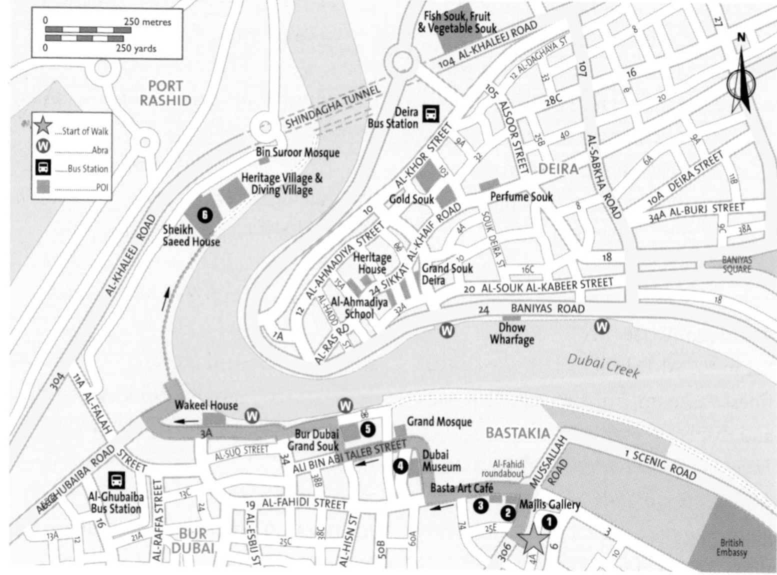

has been attractively restored. Look out for the last remaining section of town wall that has been carefully excavated and covered with a shade in one of the wider streets.

Enter the quarter from the south through the main alleyway that brings you past the Bastakiah Nights Restaurant, then loop around to the southwest corner near the roundabout.

2 Majlis Gallery

This was Dubai's first art gallery and is in a whitewashed traditional courtyard house; well worth a visit and a browse to get a feel for the local artists' talents (*see p69*).

Just a little further on, look out for the café on the same side of the road.

3 Basta Art Café

This café is also set in a traditional courtyard house within the Bastakia quarter, and makes an excellent stop for a coffee or snack (*see p163*).

Continue in a straight line along the road away from the roundabout, then bear right until you see the ship and fort of the museum in front of you.

4 Dubai Museum

Set in the Al-Fahidi fort, this is Dubai's finest museum, impressively designed and displayed (*see pp32–3*).

Head for the tall minaret of the Grand Mosque, passing the Hindu temple and going into the little lane that leads you into Bur Dubai Grand Souk.

Restaurant on the Creekside promenade

5 Bur Dubai Grand Souk

Explore the bustling bazaar area, first established in the 1830s. It is divided into sections for each trade, as is always the case in Middle Eastern souks (*see pp40–41*).

Continue to the waterfront by the abra *(crossing boat) station, and walk north around the curve of the Creek to reach the group of buildings that begin with the Sheikh Saeed House. There are also several restaurants along the Creekside where you can stop for lunch or dinner.*

6 Sheikh Saeed House

This ruler's palace has been extremely well restored as a photographic museum of Old Dubai, and the excellent air conditioning in the rooms offers welcome respite from the heat (*see pp42–3*).

THE GRAND SOUK AND WAKEEL HOUSE

As-Souk Al-Kabeer (The Grand Souk)

As-Souk Al-Kabeer is Dubai's oldest and most important souk on the Bur Dubai side of the Creek. Like the Deira Gold Souk and Spice Souk, it was established in the 1830s and is a bustling bazaar that is at its busiest at night when the heat subsides and the crowds come out. It has been the subject of a massive restoration project by the Dubai Municipality Historic Buildings Section, together with the Deira Souk areas, and over Dh30 million has been spent so far. The paving and lighting have been improved, traditional-style lanterns have been added, and the stall frontages have been given a facelift. The ugly neon signs that used to adorn many of the shops have been removed and replaced with traditional stone plaques, giving a far more traditional feel. In the entire district surrounding the souks, the Municipality is even altering specifications for modern buildings, so that advertising and signs do not mar the atmosphere.

The Grand Souk entrance in Bur Dubai

HENNA AND KOHL

In the souk look out for henna, the best-known cosmetic, which is used to dye the hair of both sexes and to paint decorations on the hands and feet of women at religious festivals and special occasions like weddings. The henna paste is made from mixing the crushed dried berries and leaves of the henna bush with medicinal herbs. Poultices of henna plant leaves are also used to treat headaches. Kohl is used as a black eyeliner, but also has medicinal properties as it helps reduce eye infections due to its mild antiseptic qualities, and it protects the eyes from dust and the sun's rays.

Originally roofed with *areesh* (palm branches) to give shade, the roof has been replaced with wood to give it more permanence because the *areesh* had to be constantly repaired and renewed after rains and high winds. The main part of the souk has a concentration of eight wind tower shops, four on each side of the main alley. Most shop owners are Indian, but a handful are still local Arab families who have always run shops in the market and whose sons wished to continue the tradition. Today, the shops sell a hotchpotch of items from jewellery, watches, clothing and silks to souvenirs and household and electrical goods.

Wakeel House

On the waterfront, close to the Bur Dubai As-Souk Al-Kabeer, is the restored Wakeel House. Purpose-built in 1934 as the office and residence of the *wakeel* (agent) of the British India Steam Navigation Company, its tower was built as a lookout from which to watch ships arriving in the Creek. The rear of the house overlooks the western entrance of the Grand Souk and the front can only be reached by boat from the Creek. The first floor was the agent's living quarters, while the ground floor housed his offices. Today, it has been designated a Marine and Diving Museum.

On the waterfront, Bur Dubai.
Open: Sat–Thur 8am–6pm.

A range of music for sale in the souk

SHINDAGHA

This is the name given to the oldest quarter of Dubai, although all of its old buildings were knocked down before any thoughts of restoration were voiced. Now, in a belated effort to put this right, the Dubai Municipality is rebuilding some 30 or so houses from scratch in Shindagha, close to Sheikh Saeed House (*see below*), in an attempt to recreate the atmosphere of Old Dubai in this totally Arab quarter where the Maktoums first settled when they broke away from Abu Dhabi.

Bin Suroor Mosque

This little mosque, built in 1930 and now set by itself in Shindagha, was last restored some years back and is now beginning to look shabby again. It is very small with just one prayer room, which makes it difficult for women to use as there is no separate place for them.

In Shindagha, beside the Heritage Village car park.

Sheikh Saeed House

Sheikh Rashid took the decision in the late 1970s to restore the house of his father Sheikh Saeed Al-Maktoum. This was the first move to restore a significant historic building in Dubai, thereby sowing the seeds for interest in restoration projects at a time when few old buildings remained, many having been bulldozed. The original building dated back to 1896 and was lived in until 1958 when Sheikh Saeed died. At that point, Sheikh Rashid moved to the Za'abil Palace, and the old palace soon fell into disrepair – buildings of this sort deteriorate quickly if they are not regularly maintained after the rainy

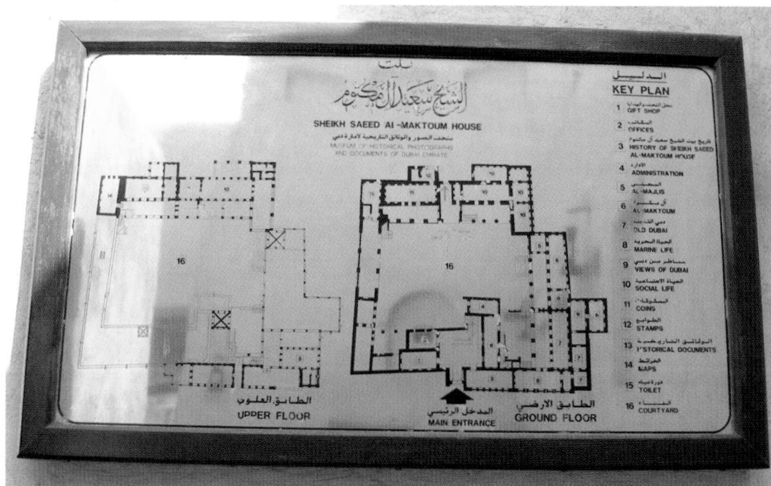

The floorplan of Sheikh Saeed House

Sheikh Saeed House is now a top tourist attraction

season. The photos inside the house show the dilapidated state of the palace before restoration work began.

The project started in 1983 and was completed in 1986. It then stood empty for ten years while it was decided what its purpose should be. Today, the house has been converted to serve as the Museum of Historical Photographs of Old Dubai, which includes pictures of the early rulers and their lifestyles, together with archival documents, maps and coins. The photographs were taken between 1948 and 1953. There is also a small exhibition room with a display about diving and the pearling industry.

In total, the house had 30 rooms, 20 verandas, 3 courtyards and 10 washrooms, and was originally divided into 6 independent living quarters for different elements of the extended family. The width of a room was never more than 2.5–3m (8–10ft) – narrow by Western standards – but this was found to be perfectly adequate when elaborate furniture was not required. A few of the upstairs rooms can be reached by both external and internal staircases. Don't miss the little entrance to the tunnel staircase on the Creekside that leads up to the *majlis* (reception room) and outdoor gallery. The *majlis*, when unlocked, has delightful views through the open shutters out onto the Creek, giving you a glimpse of how pleasurable it must have been to sit here watching the dhows pass to and fro below. The place is still as peaceful now, with an atmosphere of calm and reflection.
Al-Shindagha Rd. Open: Sat–Thur 8am–8.30pm, Fri 3–9.30pm. Admission charge.

City mosques

Mosques are the focal point of every Muslim community, and in Dubai there is a law that no one should need to walk more than 0.5km (⅓ mile) to reach one. The density of mosques is in fact higher than in many other Arab countries, and there seems to be a mosque on most street corners. Police stations, government buildings and even petrol stations have their own small mosque for employees, and each ruler's palace or residence of a wealthy owner has a private one.

The Grand Mosque in Bur Dubai

Grand Mosque

In Dubai's early days, the Grand Mosque was the centre of the town's cultural and spiritual life. It was situated between the Al-Fahidi fort (now the Dubai Museum, *see pp32–3*) and the Grand Souk in Bur Dubai (*see pp40–41*), and the same site was chosen for the new Grand Mosque, which is an enlarged version of the original. All the earliest schools, known as *kuttabs*, were part of the mosque, and children from the age of six would learn the Koran by heart there and then practise writing it. Their schooling was considered complete once they knew the Koran by heart. This task could take anything from two to five years, depending on the memory a

LEARNING BY ROTE

United Arab Emirates national Muhammad Al-Fahim recalls in his book *Rags to Riches*:

The school started early, about 6am, and lasted until noon with an hour-long breakfast break between eight and nine … Twenty-five or thirty of us sat silently reading, each struggling over a different page of the Koran … There was no question of progressing to a new page until we had completely mastered the one which preceded it.

BURIAL OF THE DEAD

Some mosques, such as the one on Al-Wasl Road in Umm Suqeim, have cemeteries attached. These are simple places where the burial spot is marked only with a stone for the head and the foot. The funeral itself is a quick affair without ceremony because the deceased must be buried within 24 hours of death.

child was blessed with. Such mosques were generally built by wealthy individuals rather than by the ruler or the community.

No hierarchy

Islam has no ecclesiastical hierarchy – one of its most attractive features – and the many mosques are not linked by any supervisory body. The custom was to lead families to build local mosques for their own use and for the use of the neighbourhood. Some property (*waqf*) was generally attached to the mosque to bring in income to pay for its maintenance. In towns, this is usually a row of shops rented out to local merchants. The rent is used to pay the salary of the muezzin (prayer leader) and for the cleaning and maintenance of the mosque. Non-Muslims do not generally enter mosques here unless invited.

Jumeirah Mosque

The elaborate Jumeirah Mosque stands on the Jumeirah Beach Road close to the Jumeirah Spinneys Centre, and is Dubai's most admired mosque from the outside. The curious hotchpotch of proportions that has resulted from Indian architects borrowing designs from Egypt, Syria, Jordan and Turkey produces a pleasing final effect.

Open: Thur & Sun mornings at 10am for a 1-hour guided tour.

The Jumeirah Mosque is Dubai's most beautiful mosque

HERITAGE VILLAGE AND DIVING VILLAGE

Heritage Village

This is a recreation of traditional village and Bedouin life, arranged as a collection of fully furnished *barasti* (palm frond) huts, some of them decked out with flooring as simple homes, some of them used as stalls selling handmade crafts. There is also a traditional coffee house with hubble-bubble water-pipes, and a small souk, with over 20 shops selling traditional handicrafts, Bedouin jewellery and pottery, and traditional medicine.

Many of the handicrafts are in fact made in India, but there are moves afoot to try to introduce more Islamic souvenirs. There are also camels and donkeys for children to ride, and the Folklore Yard in between the Heritage Village and the Diving Village is used by folk dance groups and musicians to give open-air performances.

HERBAL MEDICINES

Over the centuries, the Bedouin developed knowledge of the various medicinal properties of plants and herbs that grow wild in the desert. The desert squash (*Citrullus colocynthis*), for example, was used as a cure for diabetes, with four seeds a day said to be enough to control diabetes in the elderly. The poisonous sap of the Sodom's Apple tree (*Calotropis procera*) was dried and used to fill aching teeth. The leaves were made into poultices to heal rheumatic joints as well as being used for fertiliser, dug into the roots of ailing palm trees. Some plants were used as snuff to clear the sinuses, while others were used to cure fevers or even to dry out burns so that no scar was left behind.

The whole area along the Creekside here has been landscaped and paved, equipped with benches, waste bins and even public toilets, a great rarity in the Arab world. This makes it an attractive promenade that links up to the entrance of the Bur Dubai Grand

A typical fishing boat in the Heritage Village

Dubai's maritime history is recreated in the Diving Village

Souk, 1km (2/3 mile) away (*see pp40–41*). As in all such villages, food figures large, with many types of bread prepared by local women as you wait. There is also a big seafood restaurant. A playground area gives children the opportunity to learn to play games from earlier times.

Diving Village

This has an aquarium together with a display of all the marine equipment that was used for pearl diving in the pre-oil days, including models of different types of fishing boats. There is a diving souk selling fishing tools and instruments. During the Shopping Festival (*see pp20–21*), the place is especially lively, with fresh oysters collected daily and opened in front of you. If you are lucky, you could find a pearl worth Dh60,000. Demonstrations are held here on how to rig a dhow correctly.

Located at the head of the Creek on the Bur Dubai side between the Shindagha Tunnel and Sheikh Saeed House, the traditional-style Heritage and Diving Villages are set side by side. Open: evenings only in the hot summer months; Oct–Apr 8am–11pm. Extensive parking has been provided, accessible as you approach from the Falcon roundabout towards Shindagha Tunnel, filtering off to the right before the tunnel.

The Creek at Al-Boom is a tranquil place for a leisurely coffee

AL-BOOM TOURIST VILLAGE AND RAS AL-KHOR WILDLIFE SANCTUARY

Al-Boom Tourist Village

Al-Boom is an ambitious project based on dhows and the Creek. It operates 9 dhows on the Creek, with a capacity ranging from 20–300 passengers. The smallest one is known as *Al-Taweel* (*The Long*) and is a single-decker dhow with a capacity of 20, costing around Dh600 an hour to rent. The largest one is called *Al-Mumtaz* (*The Excellent*), a double-decker space with a capacity of 300 passengers and costing Dh4,000 to rent. The dinner cruises offer a range of international menus, and late-night trips can be arranged after dinner from around 10.30pm–midnight. *Al-Mumtaz* is a handmade 40-year-old dhow originally called *Al-Boom* (*The Owl*), from which the village takes its name. It was formerly moored outside the British Consulate.

The village also has a 15-storey hotel under construction resembling two racing dhows in full sail. It will have

DHOW CONSTRUCTION

Beyond Garhoud Bridge is the dhow construction yard at Al-Jadaf on the Bur Dubai side. New boats are still built here, while old ones decay picturesquely on the bank. Teak for dhow building is imported from India, Pakistan and Burma, and the traditional method is used whereby the outside is built with planks by eye, and the frame inserted later. This is the opposite of the Western method where the ribs are built first, then the exterior planking. Further on is the Gulf Dry Dock for ship repairs.

On the Deira bank opposite, a public jet-ski area has grown up, and on Fridays the Creek is alive with the buzzing of these exciting toys whizzing around and around, trying not to crash into each other.

150 rooms and a top-floor royal suite. There is also a café partly submerged in the Creek, plus shops, swimming pools and a marina, and in the village there are ballrooms and conference halls. On Fridays, there is a fishing competition with prizes.

Located beside Garhoud Bridge on the Bur Dubai side of the Creek, sandwiched between Creekside Park and Wonderland Water Park. www.alboom.ae

Ras Al-Khor Wildlife Sanctuary

The local jet-skiing is not compatible with the remainder of the inland part of the Creek which forms the Ras Al-Khor (Head of the Creek) Wildlife Sanctuary, mainly for the flamingos. Yet remarkably, flamingos still stop over on their migrations southwards, and a special flamingo island has been constructed with artificial nest mounds to encourage them to stay and breed. There are three bird hides, complete with binoculars allowing controlled access to the site for birdwatchers. Anti-pollution drives are in full swing, and regular dredging takes place to bring out thousands of kilograms of rubbish consisting of anything from cans and bottles to dead animals and refrigerators. There are two inspection vessels that work around the clock, in shifts, in an attempt to prevent people dumping rubbish in the Creek. The water is monitored regularly and pollution levels are said to be within safe limits at present.

Nearby at Nad Al-Sheba is the **Falconry Centre**, an excellent museum dedicated to explaining the intricacies of this Arabian sport.

Ras Al-Khor Wildlife Sanctuary. Tel: 206 4240. www.wildlife.ae. Open: hours vary. Falconry Centre. Muscat Rd. Open: daily 9am–5pm.

Flamingos at Ras Al-Khor Wildlife Sanctuary

Drive: Around Dubai

If you have rented a car and want to get a feel for the size and layout of the city, then the following circular tour will give you a flavour of what is on offer.

Depending on how long you stop at each of the places mentioned, the drive will take between 3 and 4 hours to return to the starting point.

The drive covers a total distance of some 60km (37 miles).

1 Dubai Hilton Hotel

Located some 30km (19 miles) west of the Creek, the Dubai Hilton offers competitive car hire rates and is a good starting point from which to do a quick tour of Dubai Marina, known as Al-Mina Al-Siyahi (The Tourist Port). *Drive east along the coastal road called Al-Sufouh Road, passing Dubai Media City and Dubai Internet City, heading towards the tower of Burj Al-Arab. At the traffic lights where the shopping and leisure complex of Souk Madinat Jumeirah appears to the left like a traditional village, bear left to Burj Al-Arab Hotel.*

2 Burj Al-Arab Hotel

This iconic landmark is the ultimate symbol of Dubai. Its design, as one of the world's tallest hotels at 321m (1,053ft), resembles the billowing sail

of a dhow, and it stands on its own artificial island. It is Dubai's most luxurious hotel, boasting 202 duplex suites (*see pp79, 82*). Entry is by reservation only.

Continue past the Wild Wadi Water Park and the Jumeirah Beach Hotel (built in the shape of a wave), and on past the colourful Italianate Mercato shopping mall on your right until you see the twin minarets of the Jumeirah Mosque.

3 Jumeirah Mosque

The elegantly decorated beige stonework of this mosque is the main local landmark (*see p45*).

The Burj Al-Arab is a Dubai icon

Open: Thur & Sun mornings at 10am for a 1-hour guided tour.

Continue on the coast road past Port Rashid, and go through the Shindagha Tunnel to cross the Creek. On leaving the tunnel, follow the signs for the Fish and Fruit and Vegetable Souks.

4 Fresh food souks

These souks give an excellent insight into local lifestyles and are also very easy for parking. However, you may need a strong stomach for the Fish Souk.

Now follow the signs for the Corniche, and continue along the Deira side of the Creek, past the Maktoum Bridge, turning onto the Garhoud Bridge just after the Dubai Creek Golf and Yacht Club. Follow signs back towards the coast and turn onto the Sheikh Zayed Highway to see Burj Khalifa (The Tower).

5 Burj Khalifa

Formerly known as Burj Dubai, this is the world's tallest building at over 828m (2,716ft). The American architect Adrian Smith based his design on flowers and Islamic geometric shapes to create a spiral effect. The corridor of skyscrapers that lines this section of the Sheikh Zayed Highway is like some vision of the future. Renamed after Sheikh Khalifa when the Abu Dhabi ruler gave Dubai a handout to pay its debts, it opened in early 2010. Attached is the Dubai Mall, the world's largest (*see p52*), and the Dubai Fountain, with displays every half-hour.

Shopping malls

Dubai is a shrine to shopping. Shopping is probably the national pastime, followed by sport. Dubai used to be a centre for pirate music, films and software, but this has been severely clamped down on. The biggest and glitziest of the malls are usually open from 10am–10pm daily, and are at their most crowded in the evenings when locals emerge to sit in the cafés or just to mill about in family groups.

The malls have become places not just for shopping, but for people of all ages and cultures to meet, eat and escape the climate in a cool, air-conditioned, dust-free environment, and many have cinemas and other entertainment. There is definitely a mall culture here in Dubai, and the malls have established their own individual identities. The more remarkable ones are mentioned here.

Necklaces galore

The Dubai Mall

Part of the Burj Khalifa complex, the world's biggest retail and entertainment centre has over 1,000 shops and 150 food outlets. It also has an ice rink, aquarium and underwater zoo, and access to the 124th floor of Burj Khalifa, with its spectacular viewing platform. *Downtown. Tel: 362 7500.*

Ibn Battuta Mall

Named after the 14th-century Arab explorer who spent his life travelling through the Middle East and Asia, this extraordinary mall is certainly the most beautiful and visually striking from the inside. The long, thin mall has an educational flavour and is divided into six geographical zones – China, India, Egypt, Tunisia, Andalusia and Persia – each elaborately designed to reflect that culture, with displays explaining the history and key historical figures of each region. Even the starlit sky is supplied. *Emirates Hills. Tel: 362 1900.*

Mall of the Emirates

Famous for its incorporated ski slope that stands out as a futuristic ramp when viewed from the outside, this mall was once the biggest in Dubai. Walking around its 400 outlets can easily take all day. In addition to the ski slope and the associated après-ski outlets and cafés, the mall houses the Dubai Community Arts Theatre and a new **Kempinski Hotel** (*tel: 340 1624; www.kempinski-dubai.com*). It is anchored by a gigantic Carrefour hypermarket, and also boasts the popular Harvey Nichols department store. Beyond the endless shopping possibilities, there is further entertainment in the form of a Cinestar cinema and a huge Magic Planet entertainment centre for the children.

Al-Barsha. Tel: 341 4747.

Mercato Mall

The most visually striking from the outside because of its Renaissance-style architecture, this compact mall offers a mere 90 outlets, but is still the largest in Jumeirah.

Jumeirah. Tel: 344 4161.

Souk Madinat Jumeirah

An astonishing recreation of a traditional souk, designed with narrow winding alleyways, this mall has many speciality shops not found elsewhere, and a unique waterway system linking its cafés, bars and restaurants.

Umm Suqeim. Tel: 366 8888.

The Italianate interior of the Mercato Mall in Jumeirah

Wafi Mall

Styled on an Egyptian theme, with its roofs in the form of the three pyramids, the Wafi Mall is Dubai's most exclusive and upmarket shopping complex, with designer boutiques and outlets specialising in haute couture and jewellery. In 2007, the latest extension added the five-star **Raffles Dubai Hotel** (*tel: 324 8888; www.raffles.com/dubai*), another 90 shops and an underground souk called Khan Murjan, with artisans' workshops creating items on site.

Umm Hurair. Tel: 324 4555.

Walk: Deira side of the Creek

Many visitors never come to the Deira side of the Creek except to visit the Gold Souk, believing there is no more to see. Yet this is the commercial heart of the old merchant community of Dubai, its narrow maze of streets alive with bustling souks selling everything from spices and perfumes to plastic brooms and brushes. Parking is extremely difficult, and traffic becomes very congested during peak rush hours; the best way to come is by taxi or by abra *(crossing boat) from the opposite bank of the Creek.*

Palm Deira

Starting at the seafront, the major landmark is the **Hyatt Regency Hotel** (*tel: 209 1234; www.dubai.regency.hyatt.com*), which dominates Deira's corniche of landscaped greenery and palm trees. Just beyond the hotel but before the Hamriya Port, work is currently on hold for the construction of the Palm Deira, the third and biggest

The Etisalat building with its distinctive golf-ball top, seen from the Creek

of the Nakheel Palm Island Projects (*see p26*). Set to cover over 80sq km (31sq miles), it is planned to be bigger than Paris or Manhattan and almost as big as Greater London. The corniche area here is also scheduled to be transformed by replacing the older buildings with new residential and commercial blocks, smart public utilities and tourist attractions.

The Deira Fish Souk has a huge selection of fish

Food souks

Between the Hyatt Regency Hotel and the Creek, signs lead off to the Fish Souk and the Fruit and Vegetable Souk, surrounded by extensive parking areas. The Fish Souk is the largest in Dubai, where the freshest fish can be bought at very cheap prices. The Dubai Municipality has recently created a **fish museum** here that gives useful information on the 350 species of fish found in the Arabian Gulf, the types of traditional fishing boats used and the history of the fishing trade in the United Arab Emirates. The Fruit and Vegetable Souk is a riot of colours with all manner of exotic produce often sold in boxes at reasonable prices. Food shopping of this sort is generally the domain of men in the Arab world, so you will not see many women here.

Heritage area

If you wander around on foot behind the Gold Souk (*see pp62–3*) you will discover the oldest part of Deira, an area known as As-Souk Al-Kabeer (the Grand Souk), which Dubai Municipality has been renovating in recent years (*see p40*).

Dhow wharfage

Take time to stroll along the Creek corniche where the colourful working dhows are moored and laden with diverse goods, from electrical wares and cars to fruit and vegetables. The crew's washing is generally strung out on lines on deck, and the photogenic dhows vary greatly in size.

Futuristic frontage

Before you get to Maktoum Bridge, the next stretch of corniche boasts some famous landmarks like the Etisalat building with its golf ball on top, the National Bank of Dubai (known locally as 'the pregnant lady') with its glass convex mirror, and three of the city's oldest five-star hotels – the Hilton Dubai Creek, the InterContinental Dubai and the Sheraton Dubai Creek (*see p161*).

BIN DALMOUK MOSQUE AND GRAND SOUK DEIRA

Bin Dalmouk Mosque

Part of the Al-Ahmadiya and Heritage House complex (*see pp60–61*), this charming little mosque built in 1930 belonged to the wealthy Lootah family. It was totally demolished before its architecture could be recorded, so it has had to be rebuilt from old photos. Traditional building materials were used throughout, and the main pillared hall is now air-conditioned, making it a blissfully cool haven on hot summer days. The mosque is in use, but may only be entered with permission and after taking off shoes.

Grand Souk Deira

This souk was Dubai's oldest and busiest, the point at which the dhows from Iran and India would unload their goods. It covers a large area between Al-Nasr Square and the Gold Souk. Today, the shops here are run mainly by Indians and they sell a variety of wares, from clothes and spices to household items. The easiest way to approach the souk is to take the *abra* (crossing boat) from the Bur Dubai side, and then from the *abra* station on the Deira side take the pedestrian underpass to the left, which brings you directly into the souk. The Spice Souk is inside.

First built in 1850, the souk has been under restoration since the 1990s, prohibiting vehicular access. Some of the shops in the Iranian section have traditional wind towers, and this part is known as Bandar Taalib Souk, dating from 1920. In the restoration work, teak wood shutters have been added to the stalls to help preserve the original atmosphere, and the paving and lighting have been carefully redone in traditional style. The ugly and inappropriately garish shop signs have gradually been replaced by tasteful carved plasterwork ones, reconstructed with the help of old photos. For rugs and carpets, your best option is the Deira Tower on Al-Nasr Square, where a concentration of around 40 shops offers a large selection from Iran, Pakistan, Turkey and Afghanistan.

DRESS CODE

Many expatriates, especially women, are strangely insensitive to their dress and the offence it causes to local people if they are too scantily clad. Skimpy shorts and T-shirts are fine within the hotels and on the beach, but they are to be avoided in public places. Long, loose dresses or skirts and tops are the best choice for foreign women, keeping the knees and elbows covered. They are also more suited to the climate, offering greater protection against the sun and skin damage. The long, loose robes worn locally by men and women did not originate because of Islam. Long before that, the people discovered that this was the most comfortable and the most protective form of dress. From the ruler right down to the poorest person, the white *dishdasha* (full-length men's robe) is worn like a uniform. The white reflects the sun, and underneath the men wear shorts or trousers, cotton socks and shoes in town, and sandals outside the town. They are never bare-headed. Children in *dishdashas* still play football and ride bikes.

Household goods for sale in the Grand Souk, Deira

Walk: Deira

Deira, the old commercial heart of Dubai, cannot be appreciated except on foot, as vehicle access is extremely difficult. It is best walked in the early morning or early evening when the heat has subsided. Many of the shops close between 1pm and 4pm, and this is no good if you want to see Deira at its bustling best. The markets are clearly signposted to the left just after emerging from the Shindagha Tunnel.

Allow 2–3 hours, longer if you plan to shop along the way. The total distance covered is about 3km (1¾ miles).

1 Fish Souk and Fruit and Vegetable Souk

This is the best starting point for the walk as parking is easy here. It introduces you to the local produce markets where you can see at first hand how Dubai locals do their shopping.

Take the pedestrian underpass to cross the main Al-Khaleej Road, pass the bus station on your right, then turn right into Al-Khor Street. Continue for 200m (220yds) until you come to the entrance of the enclosed Gold Souk, with its welcome air conditioning.

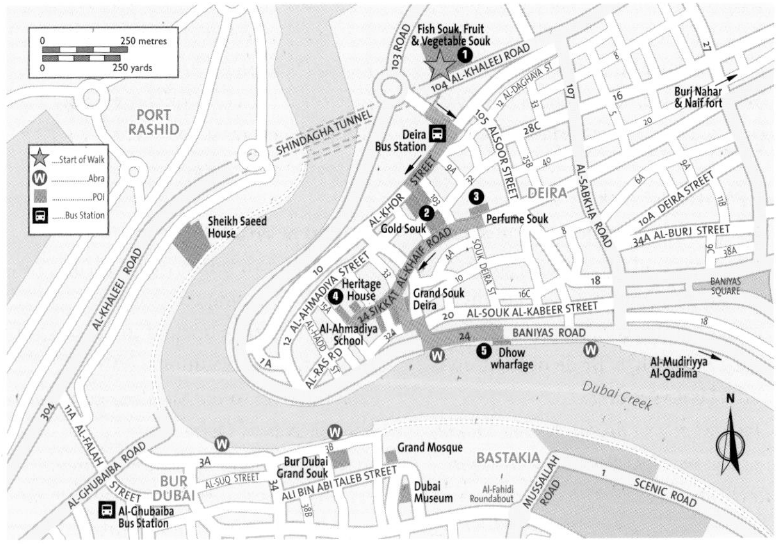

The *abra* crossing at Deira, with traditional dhows in the background

2 Gold Souk

This enormous collection of shops sells not only gold, but silver, precious stones and pearls as well (*see pp62–3*).
Walk right through to the exit on the south side and turn left onto Sikkat Al-Khaif Road. After 100m (110yds), you will come to the Perfume Souk.

3 Perfume Souk

This heady conglomeration of stalls sells every kind of perfume imaginable, but the most exciting ones are the Arabian *attars*, concentrated oils with exotic names like 'Bride of the Desert' and 'Harem's Secret'.
Double back on Sikkat Al-Khaif Road, passing the Gold Souk on your right, until after about 300m (330yds) you come to the square with Heritage House.

4 Al-Ahmadiya School and Heritage House

These attractive buildings are open daily (*Sat–Thur 8am–7.30pm, Fri 2–7.30pm. Free admission*) (*see pp60–61*).
*Retrace your steps then walk south towards the Creek corniche, passing through the Grand Souk Deira (*see p56*) to emerge at the Creek.*

5 Dhow wharfage

This stretch of the Deira corniche from the *abra* (crossing boat) station onwards offers a fascinating glimpse of the assembled traditional dhows, moored here to unload their goods into the markets of Deira.
You can pick up a taxi easily from any point along the corniche to return to the car park at the start of the walk.

AL-RAS

Al-Ahmadiya School

This school forms part of the restored complex of buildings that is located in the heart of Al-Ras (meaning 'head', that is, of the Creek), close to the Grand Souk Deira, where the wealthy traders would have lived at the beginning of the 20th century.

Dubai's earliest proper school, Al-Ahmadiya is one of the city's most pleasing architectural structures. It conveys great harmony, and the height and airiness of its rooms must have made it a pleasure to study here. The decorative elements are especially fine, with cusped arches on the ground-floor verandas, and gypsum stucco inscriptions from the Koran on the classroom doors. This delicate, intricate work takes a long time, which is why the building took four years to restore.

The elegant courtyard of Al-Ahmadiya School

Built in 1912, the school is named after its patron Sheikh Ahmad Bin Dalmouk. Dubai's wealthiest and most distinguished sons (no daughters received education at that time) were taught here by leading teachers of the day in eight classrooms.

From the 1950s, the building began to be neglected as new schools were built elsewhere. It was used by the Department of Islamic Affairs and Awqaf (Religious Endowments) for a few years, but then in the 1960s they, too, moved out to a more spacious modern building.

Beside Al-Ahmadiya on the street side is a building originally earmarked as the Museum of Traditional Architecture, built in 1880 and now Deira's Tourist Centre, while further into the heart of Deira is a group of small old huts, now restored as a series of souvenir shops.

Al-Ahmadiya Street, Deira. Open: Sat–Thur 8am–7.30pm, Fri 2–7.30pm. Free admission.

Heritage House

Fronting onto the street and joined to Al-Ahmadiya School is the impressive

LOCAL DRESS

The white full-length *dishdasha* is worn by all men, along with the *ghutra* (head cloth) in plain white or red and white checks, and the twisted black *aqaal* (coil). Under the head cloth men wear a skull cap called a *taqia*. Over the *dishdasha*, men of importance wear a black or fawn *bisht* (cloak) edged with gold. Wearing the *bisht* well requires a certain bearing. When the temperature rises, men wear Western-style jackets over the *dishdasha* on the principle of body insulation, unlike Westerners who prefer to strip. The beard is kept by men as a sign of virility and social acceptance. In the old days, the beard was plucked out as a punishment.

private house of Sheikh Ahmad Bin Dalmouk himself. It is now known as Heritage House, and restoration began in 1994, taking two years. An aesthetically pleasing structure built in 1890, it is very spacious inside with high ceilings. Especially attractive is the upstairs summer *majlis* (reception room), designed to catch the breezes from the Creek. At the time it was built, the Creek's beachfront was just in front of it with no obstructions. The decorative crenellations along the top of the walls are very striking. The rooms have been traditionally furnished to recreate their original functions, and the bride's room offers an interesting glimpse into the past. *Al-Ahmadiya Street, Deira. Open: Sat–Thur 8am–7.30pm, Fri 2–7.30pm. Free admission.*

Traditional furniture in the courtyard of Heritage House

The Gold Souk

Completely covered and air-conditioned, the Gold Souk is set in the back alleys of Deira. This is one of the largest retail gold markets in the world, and certainly in Arabia. Hundreds of small stalls sell gold from many countries, from actual ingots to finely worked jewellery, as well as silver, precious stones and pearls. The alleyways appear endless and you may find it difficult to retain your sense of direction. Evening is the best time to stroll in a leisurely fashion around the alleys, when the souk is at its liveliest, and the gold glistens in the lights.

Gold statuettes to suit all tastes

CITY OF GOLD

Dubai promotes itself as the City of Gold and since 1997 it has become the world's largest gold distribution centre, having overtaken Singapore. The United Arab Emirates and Saudi Arabia have the world's highest per capita annual consumption of gold, at 15g (1/2oz). The country's total annual demand, including items for re-export, exceeds 350 tonnes. Dubai's gold is imported from 16 countries, led by Switzerland, then the UK, then South Africa. Dubai's main export markets are Japan, India, South Korea, Taiwan, Switzerland, the UK, the USA, Oman, Thailand and Germany. Dubai gold prices are on average 18 per cent cheaper than Hong Kong and 40–50 per cent lower than in most European countries.

Throughout the Gulf and the subcontinent, a bride's dowry must contain gold, and tradition has it that the bride's gold must be new, a practice that guarantees a steady flow of customers as families haggle for the best prices for their daughters' dowries. The range available is colossal, from earrings, finger, toe and nose rings to necklaces, chains, bracelets, anklets, amulets and

A typical shop window in the Gold Souk

elaborate headdresses only worn once, on the bride's wedding day.

You can also commission items to be made if you have at least a week to spare, and you can specify the colour of gold you prefer – from the pinker, yellower, whiter or greener shades.

It is now easier to visit the market since the introduction of the metered car park opposite its entrance. Open: Sat–Thur 10am–10pm, Fri 4–10pm. The shops stay open until 10pm or later depending on season and trade. Note that many of the shops close between 1pm and 4pm, so this time is best avoided.

PROVERBS OF ARABIA

To understand a people, acquaint yourself with their proverbs:

- The man who cheats you once will cheat you 100 times.
- If a man criticises the merchandise it is because he wants to buy it.
- Too soft and you will be squeezed, too hard and you will be broken.
- There is no messenger like money.
- Marriage is like a castle under siege: those within want to get out, those outside want to get in.
- The beauty of a man is in his intelligence; the intelligence of a woman is in her beauty.
- Three things prolong life: a big house, a swift horse and an obedient wife.
- The pleasure of food and drink lasts an hour, of sleep a day, of women a month, but of a building a lifetime.

Deira Spice Souk

A wander through Deira's old Spice Souk, set within the narrow streets and winding alleyways of the Grand Souk Deira, gives you an opportunity to experience the Dubai of old, a million miles away from the futuristic skyscrapers and hectic pace of the modern city. The number of shops selling spices is gradually diminishing under the pressure of convenience shopping in the mall hypermarkets, most of which have rival spice stalls within their food sections. However, the malls cannot offer the same thrill as that of buying from an authentic outlet with an Indian stall owner who knows the business and is only too happy to offer advice on the various spices and their uses. The spices are generally still displayed in the same sacks in which they were unloaded from the dhows to preserve their absolute freshness, and the heady aromas of cardamom, cinnamon, cumin and cloves fill the air. Try some of the *zaatar*, a local form of wild thyme, often sprinkled on freshly baked bread. As well as the spices themselves, the sacks displayed outside the shop fronts also contain herbs, nuts, dried fruits, chillies and pulses. Inside, the shelves have bottles of rose water and orange water, henna powders to colour the hair and kohl for eyeliner – all Arab specialities that have been used for generations.

Stall owners will gladly give a demonstration of how to use frankincense, and they also sell the clay incense burners that come in all shapes and sizes, along with the coals. Local people use frankincense regularly and pass the smoking incense burner among their guests so that the exotic aromas can perfume the clothes and hair.

The colourful variety of spices on sale in the Deira Spice Souk

A bag of frankincense at the Spice Souk

FRANKINCENSE

Probably the most popular purchase is frankincense, displayed in sackfuls according to quality. The best crystals come from Dhofar in southern Oman, where the resinous sap is bled from the local frankincense trees. The further the trees are from the coast, the higher the quality of the resin. The harvesting can only take place between March and August, when cuts are made into the tree bark allowing the resin to seep out and coagulate into semi-opaque lumps over a three- to five-day period.

A much-sought-after substance, frankincense was more valuable than gold in the time of Christ, and was used in religious rites, where it was burnt as incense, and for medicinal purposes in most civilisations throughout the ancient world. It has even been suggested that frankincense was the first commodity that led to the idea of international trade routes, and that the Queen of Sheba, for whom Dhofar was a colony, visited King Solomon in Jerusalem purely in order to agree a safe caravan route. Frankincense burns well thanks to its high oil content and is an essential part of weddings, *eid* festivities and birth celebrations. An exotic version of frankincense called *bakhour* is produced by mixing it with other aromatic substances such as *oudh* (scented wood from India), sandalwood, myrrh and rose water. All the ingredients are cooked, dried and then ground down into a powder for burning on coals.

AL-QUSAIS, BURJ NAHAR AND NAIF FORT

Al-Qusais archaeological site

This site is Dubai's most important in archaeological terms because of the rich finds in the graves here. The site is officially closed, but the three tombs found here were dated between 2500 BC and 1500 BC. The nearby Mound of the Serpents, which yielded the richest finds, has now disappeared or at any rate cannot be found because the excavators of the 1970s left inadequate records. The hole has been extensively built over with the growth of the city, and the chances of being able to trace the original site are slim. The mound acquired its name from the many models of bronze snakes unearthed here which, together with hundreds of bronze arrowheads, tiny bronze daggers, vases and bowls with snakes moulded onto them, suggested it was some kind of ritual site with offerings, the snake having long been associated with immortality in ancient legend because of its ability to shed its skin and emerge as new. The snakes and all the grave finds are on display in the Dubai Museum (*see pp32–3*). *North of Dubai International Airport off the Sharjah Highway.*

***MAJLIS* SYSTEM**

This simple but effective system of government existed throughout the Gulf for centuries and was still in use until the 1960s. Each sheikh held his own *majlis* or council (literally 'place of sitting') to which any member of the tribe could come with their grievances.

Burj Nahar

Built around 1870, the Nahar tower was one in a line of defences to the east and north of the city, along with Al-Baraha Tower built in 1910. Burj Nahar now stands incongruously by

Burj Nahar, one of three watchtowers guarding the old city

A traditional dhow for hire on the Creek

itself in Deira's business district, surrounded by a small garden.
Omar Ibn Al-Khattab Street, Deira.

Naif fort

The Naif fort was one of the city's oldest defences, serving for many years as a police station. Since 1995, it has been extensively restored to resemble the original fort, although the only structure remaining is the tower itself. The new police station houses the **Police Museum** on the ground floor, which is open to the public, alongside all the normal police offices, like the criminal investigation department (CID).
Southern side of Naif Road, just to the left (west) of the Naif roundabout.

Al-Mudiriyya Al-Qadima (Old Municipality Building)

This corner building dating to 1950, with its green-painted overhanging first-floor balcony and roof, makes an interesting contrast to the huge red marble building that is further east along Deira Creekside and today serves as the Dubai Municipality. Nowadays, the Old Municipality Building is a corner shop called Latifi Stores.
Set on the Deira Creekfront just a short way before (east of) Grand Souk Deira.

RECREATING HISTORY

Since almost everything of any age in Dubai was bulldozed or allowed to fall into disrepair after oil was discovered in the 1950s, the emirate is in the unfortunate or, depending on your viewpoint, fortunate position of having to recreate history and traditional culture. This is not specifically for the benefit of tourists, but for Dubai's own youth, the under-25s, who have only known life here since oil wealth. The necessity to illustrate life as it was lived pre-1960 is a wonderful opportunity, a sort of carte blanche to write history from an entirely controlled standpoint.

A collection of antiques for sale in a Dubai antique shop

GALLERIES

Sharjah used to be the undoubted cultural heart of the emirates, but this is changing fast and Dubai now boasts a flourishing art scene with increasing numbers of galleries springing up.

Art Space

A glamorous contemporary gallery with new exhibitions every month and champagne opening nights, Art Space is run by young curators dedicated to nurturing local talent. It has shown pop art by Emirati artists and powerful images by female Iranian artists.
Located at Fairmont on the Sheikh Zayed Highway. Tel: 323 0820. www.artspace-dubai.com

Creative Art Centre

This is a large gallery and shop with eight showrooms offering a wide range of original art, framed maps and antiques, including Omani chests and old carved wooden doors, old weapons and silver. The gallery specialises in antiques restoration.
Located in Jumeirah, set back from the Beach Road between Choithrams supermarket and the Town Centre shopping mall. Tel: 349 6444.

Four Seasons Ramesh Gallery

Specialising in photography, this gallery originally opened in 1970. It exhibits and sells work by both local and international artists, with interesting photos of Dubai's history.
Set in one end of the large store in Block A of Al-Zomorrodah Building on Zabeel Road. Tel: 334 9090. www.fourseasonsgallery.com

Green Art Gallery

This gallery holds exhibitions between October and May. Its speciality is work inspired by the local heritage and culture, and it has a large collection of original art, limited edition prints and hand-crafted work by local artists.

Housed in Villa 23, Street 51, behind Dubai Zoo. Tel: 349 6444. Open: Oct–end May.

Majlis Gallery

This is Dubai's oldest gallery and it is set within a beautifully restored and whitewashed courtyard house. It offers a series of exhibitions, each usually lasting about ten days, and although it is run as a commercial gallery to promote art and artefacts of an international standard, it always welcomes anyone with an interest in the house itself. You can drop in and enjoy the atmosphere of tranquillity and calm. Before it opened to the public in 1989, it was for ten years the home of an English family, the first Westerners to settle in the Bastakia quarter. The gallery exhibits mainly paintings, Islamic calligraphy and sculpture by local artists, as well as some items of pottery, ceramics, glassware and even furniture.

Located in a whitewashed courtyard house on Al-Fahidi Street, just off the Al-Fahidi roundabout on the edge of the Bastakia quarter. Tel: 353 6233. www.themajlisgallery.com

Third Line

One of the most adventurous in Dubai, this gallery has presented challenging contemporary work that dares to break the boundaries of the traditional arts, such as Islamic calligraphy and Persian miniatures, creating entirely new forms.

In Al-Quoz, off the Sheikh Zayed Highway at Interchange 3, next to The Courtyard. Tel: 341 1367. www.thethirdline.com

XVA Gallery

This, one of Dubai's most interesting galleries, is set in a restored wind tower house in the middle of Bastakia. It focuses on paintings, both local and international, and hosts many exhibitions throughout the year. There is a shaded café in the tranquil courtyard and eight guest rooms on the upper floors, with a roof terrace and rocking chairs.

Building 7, Gate Village, Zabeel Road. Tel: 358 5117. www.xvagallery.com

An example of Dubai art

City parks

Dubai Municipality has a 'greenification' policy and is committed to creating as much green space as possible. The hope is that, apart from improving the look of the landscape along the roadsides, this will keep pollution at bay as the number of cars on the roads increases, since the trees absorb the carbon dioxide of the exhaust fumes and release oxygen instead. Many of the city parks have days when they are open for women and children only, and all charge admission.

Creekside Park

Although in a fine Creekside setting, no swimming is permitted in the Creek water at this park. The park stretches for 2.5km (1½ miles) between the Floating Bridge and Garhoud Bridge on the Bur Dubai side. There is parking for 900 cars, and besides the usual restaurant and kiosk facilities there is even an 18-hole mini-golf course, a children's playground and a train that does a circuit of the park (*trains tend not to run noon–4pm*). Like all parks in Dubai, there are public toilets and cool water dispensers at intervals throughout.

Open: Sat–Wed 8am–9.30pm, Thur & Fri 8am–10.30pm. No pets or bicycles, and no football or barbecues on the grass.

Traditional *barasti* shading is provided by the Municipality

Jumeirah Beach Park

This park is extensively used by Russian visitors to Dubai who are shipped in by the busload. Notices have even been erected in Russian giving the park rules. The park is attractively landscaped with wooden steps down onto the beach, which is well equipped with showers but no changing rooms. There is a children's playground and a designated picnic and barbecue area.
Open: 8am–11pm. Mon: women and children only.

Mushrif Park

Set 15km (9 miles) outside the city beyond the airport, this is a wilder, less manicured park of 125ha (309 acres), featuring a unique World Village.
Open: 8am–11pm. Admission charge with car. No pets, bikes or football in the park.

Safa Park

Probably the most popular park with resident expatriates, this 64ha (158-acre) green space is one of Dubai's oldest, established in 1975. Set in Jumeirah, the park spans the gap between Al-Wasl Road and the Sheikh Zayed Highway. There are three entrances, and cars must be left outside in the designated parking areas. There is a big wheel, a dodgem area and a roundabout, together with an indoor air-conditioned gaming hall. Tandem or four-seater bicycles can be hired for adults, but children under ten will have trouble reaching the pedals. There are children's playgrounds scattered everywhere and in the centre is a landscaped hill and lake area with pedal boats for hire. Grouped together are three model gardens – Dubaian, European and Oriental – and there is also a small maze in a separate area.

The big wheel at Safa Park

Unlike other parks, Safa Park has a tennis court, a football pitch, volleyball and basketball, as well as jogging and fitness circuits. Walking and jogging around the perimeter of the park are popular expatriate activities in the early morning and evening.
Open: Sat–Wed 6.30am–9.30pm (Tue: women only), Thur & Fri 7.30am–10.30pm. Admission charge. No pets or bicycles, and no football or barbecues on the grass.

Walk: Al-Mamzar Park and the seafront

At 99ha (245 acres), Al-Mamzar is easily Dubai's largest beach park. It has the advantage of being on a promontory surrounded on three sides by the sea. A visit is quite expensive, so you are likely to want to stay for at least half a day to make it worthwhile. There are four well-maintained beaches and three swimming pools. Bicycles can be rented and there is a train tour. The walk covers 2–3km (1¼–2 miles) and takes around an hour.

Open: Sat–Wed 8am–9.30pm (Wed: women and children only), Thur & Fri 8am–10.30pm. Admission charges are per car, including all occupants, or per person on foot.

From the Deira Corniche, follow the signs to Al-Mamzar Park to reach the main entrance. There is parking for 1,200 cars outside the park and for 460 inside for those using the pools and the beach chalets. Enter and pay at the main entrance. From there, follow the waymarked paths to the amphitheatre.

1 Amphitheatre

The amphitheatre is located near the entrance, and during the Dubai Shopping Festival there are special activities organised here, as well as shows for children. The fine views out to sea from the top have now been somewhat marred by the offshore construction of the Palm Deira to the west. The eastern side of the park is flanked by its own creek, Khor Al-Mamzar, which forms the border with Sharjah.

Follow the park signs to the Traditional Café in the centre of the park.

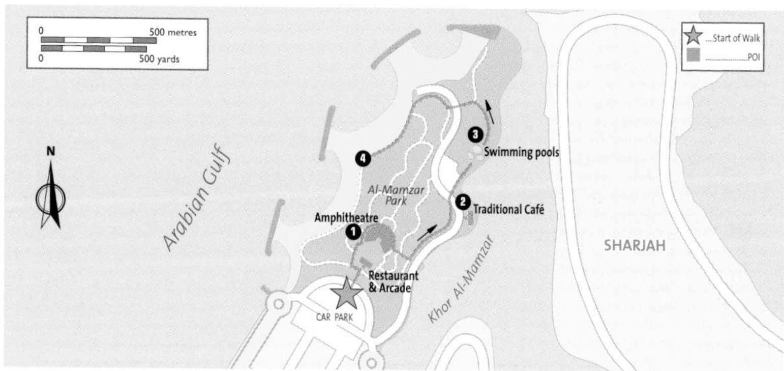

2 Traditional Café

Built largely of *barasti* (palm fronds), this café makes a fine centrepiece and offers welcome shade. There are a further 12 fast-food and drink kiosks scattered throughout the park. The paths wind through plentiful picnic areas and children's playgrounds.
Follow the signs to the swimming pools.

3 Swimming pools

Al-Mamzar Park is unique in Dubai because it has swimming pools, fully equipped with showers and changing rooms, and the pools themselves have water slides. Reassuringly, there are also lifeguards on patrol.
Follow the signs to the beach.

4 Beaches

The four beaches here are well kept and clean, and there are showers and changing rooms at regular intervals along the shoreline. There are even air-conditioned chalets with their own barbecue area for rent by the day.

DATE PALM

One of the diet staples throughout the Arabian Peninsula, dates are on average 70 per cent sugar (excluding the stones), which prevents the growth of bacteria and enables dates to stay edible for long periods in a hostile climate, unlike any other tropical fruit. The date was, therefore, an essential item at sea during the pearling season, along with limes and fish. Apart from its food value, the branches, fibre, leaves and trunk of the date palm formed the basic building material for houses and shelters in the past, for fish traps in the days before metal and nylon, and even for fans and toys. They are now used for sacks, bags and matting. The Prophet Muhammad's first mosque at Medina in AD 630 used palm trunks for the beams and columns, the branches for roofing and the leaves for prayer mats.

Date palms reach heights of up to 30m (100ft) and the clusters contain around 200 dates

DUBAI ZOO

The controversial Dubai Zoo began life in the 1960s as the private collection of Otto J Bulart, an animal-lover who had come to Dubai in 1962 to make underwater films. On the roof of the buildings where he lived in Deira, he began collecting animals from all sorts of places, some given by local people. His cow was given by the ruler, Sheikh Rashid. When the collection reached the point of bursting from the rooftops, Sheikh Rashid granted him 2ha (5 acres) of land in Jumeirah, which is the site of today's zoo. The space was generous for a private collection, but once it evolved into a full-blown zoo at the insistence of Bulart's patrons, with creatures like giraffes, lions and tigers, it became far too cramped. In 1971, the zoo was appropriated by the Dubai Municipality.

DANGER FROM VISITORS

The overcrowding problems in Dubai Zoo are exacerbated by the many visitors who clearly have no understanding of the animals or their needs. They throw stones at the animals to make them move, taunt them, and feed them unsuitable food and bits of rubbish. On occasion, this has resulted in the death of some animals, like the emu that was found, on being cut open, to have a baby's dummy blocking its gut. The number of visitors is increasing, with over 400,000 a year, and the animals are more at risk from the visitors than the other way around.

Breeding programmes

From 1971, the zoo was managed by various people until Dr Reza Khan from

The old zoo is bursting at the seams

Birds such as these cockatoos thrive in the zoo's aviary

Al-Ain Zoo took the reins in 1989. He built the very successful aviaries, and the African spoonbill has bred here even though it rarely breeds in captivity. He has also succeeded in breeding the Socotra cormorant, making him the first successful breeder in the world of these, and he has donated pairs to Kuwait and Riyadh Zoos. The zoo actively participates in animal exchange programmes for breeding, and is the only one in the Arab world so far to have successfully bred chimps, Nile crocodiles and African turtles. The zoo has also bred Arabian wolves, which are on the verge of extinction in Arabia because of urban sprawl. Like the Arabian leopard (*see p147*), they have been hunted by farmers who see them as a threat to their cattle and poultry.

Overcrowding

There are now 1,200 animals in the 2ha (5-acre) space, many of which were not solicited but sent to the zoo for housing by the authorities, having been confiscated at the airport from irresponsible animal dealers. The zoo has become a sort of haven for illicitly smuggled animals, or even for animals that are just mysteriously happened upon. One man even brought in a cobra – complete with fangs – in a biscuit tin. The overcrowding will continue until the zoo is given the go-ahead to move to new premises, but so far none of the schemes for this have ever got beyond the planning stage.

Jumeirah. Open: Wed–Mon 10am–6pm. Closed: Tue. Admission charge.

The Dubai World Cup

This is the annual world championship horse race run over 2km (1¼ miles) on sand, the personal creation of Sheikh Muhammad in the 1990s. The race immediately caught the world's attention by offering huge prize money, currently $10 million, tax-free, plus excellent facilities for the horses and their entourages at Meydan. The veterinary clinic here, run by an American and set up by Sheikh Muhammad, is one of the most sophisticated in the world. The inaugural race was watched in 197 different countries and covered in leading international papers.

All the stops are pulled out for this annual event

THE HORSE IN ARABIA

Horse racing, much patronised by the ruling sheikhs, is fast becoming the most lucrative and exciting spectator sport in Dubai. Renowned as it is in Arabic literature, the horse was in fact a relatively late import to the Arabian Peninsula. It was not known to the early Semites, but having been domesticated by nomadic Indo-European herdsmen east of the Caspian Sea in early antiquity, it was imported by the Hittites of Turkey and then into Syria. From Syria, the horse was introduced into Arabia some time shortly before Christ and, once there, it had the best chance to keep its blood pure and free from admixture because very few foreign forces invaded Arabia. The ancient horse fossils found in Abu Dhabi belonged to a quite different, now extinct, animal called Hipparion, a small pony with three toes on each hoof. The Arabian thoroughbred is renowned for its physical beauty, endurance, intelligence and touching devotion to its master. Unsuited to the desert, the horse is an animal of luxury, and its feeding and care is a difficult matter for the desert-dweller. Until the early 20th century, its possession was a sign of wealth, and the horse's chief value was in providing the necessary speed for a successful Bedouin raid. The horse was also used in hunting and sporting tournaments, and today Sheikh Muhammad continues the tradition of endurance races up to 120km (75 miles) that are completed in less than eight hours. The Sheikh's own son Rashid has even set records in such races.

The new facilities at Meydan in Nad Al-Sheba, near Ras Al-Khor, opened in 2010 and include a fine grandstand overlooking the immaculately kept grounds; they are being continually improved, as is the prize money for the race-goers. One year, the public was invited to try to select all six winners, for a prize of 1kg (2¼lb) of gold. Since Islam does not permit gambling, the race-goers fill in 'forecast sheets'. Sheikh Muhammad capped it all on one occasion when his own horse Singspiel won the Cup, thereby saving himself a great deal of prize money. He also flies in celebrities of his choice to lend additional glamour to the event. The total cost of staging the event is reckoned to be around US$15 million.

Racing takes place throughout the winter months from October to April, with top jockeys from Australia, Europe and the USA regularly competing. There are usually six or seven races in an evening, starting at 7pm (or 9pm during Ramadan) under floodlights. Free admission. Dress code is casual for the public enclosures, and smart-casual in the clubhouse and private viewing boxes.

The glittering prize that awaits the winner

JUMEIRAH, UMM SUQEIM AND THE SUBURBS

These are the expensive residential suburbs that extend west from the Jumeirah Mosque out to the iconic Burj Al-Arab Hotel. In order of desirability, Jumeirah still tops the bill, followed by Umm Suqeim, Al-Sufouh and Al-Barsha.

Dubai's suburbs are finally stalling

Jumeirah

The true area of Jumeirah is a prime 9km (5½-mile) strip of coastline running west from Port Rashid, but the name has been widely hijacked because of its upmarket connotations. Even the Palm Jumeirah is actually offshore from Al-Sufouh, not Jumeirah. The rents for the villas here are the highest in Dubai. Most of the British schools are in this area. Standing on the Beach Road, the Jumeirah Mosque, with its elegant twin minarets, is the district's best known landmark.

JUMEIRAH ARCHAEOLOGICAL SITE

This extensive 6th-century AD camel caravan site lies today in the heart of the developed residential district of Jumeirah, just inland from the Jumeirah Beach Park. First excavated by the American University of Beirut from 1969–70 and then by the Iraqis in 1975, Dubai's own local team of archaeologists has been working on the site more recently. Built a century before the coming of Islam, and contemporary with the Persian Sassanian culture, the series of stone walls that showed above ground was excavated to reveal a souk with a number of shops, a few stone-built houses and a large courtyard house thought to be the governor's palace, elegantly decorated with Persian-style sculpted plaster. One other large building was excavated, which the archaeologists eventually identified as a hunting lodge. It was used for two or three centuries in all, and is the only site in the United Arab Emirates to span the pre-Islamic and Islamic periods.

Umm Suqeim

Slightly cheaper than Jumeirah, this area is popular with expatriates because it is well placed for local schools, served by the new Spinneys Centre for shopping, close to the beach, and equidistant to the Creek and the new Dubai emerging further west along the coast towards the marina.

Al-Sufouh

This suburb stretches between Umm Suqeim and the Dubai Marina; it is the new up-and-coming district thanks to the Palm Jumeirah development just offshore. Secondary education is well served here, with Dubai College and the American University of Dubai, as well as the new Knowledge City and Internet City. Al-Sufouh is all villas and Dubai Marina is all apartments, the latter being the first freehold development in the United Arab Emirates where many far-sighted expatriates bought purely for the investment.

Al-Barsha

This is the residential area inland from Al-Sufouh, close to the Mall of the Emirates. It consists mainly of large independent villas, with three to five bedrooms. About 75 per cent are lived in by locals, with expatriates renting the remainder. It is very well placed for those working in Media City and Internet City, and is a quiet and safe area.

One of the exclusive expat villas in Jumeirah

BURJ AL-ARAB AND JEBEL ALI

Burj Al-Arab Hotel

Consciously built as the iconic symbol of Dubai, the Burj Al-Arab Hotel was the boldest and most ambitious of the many projects initiated in the 1990s under the direct guidance of Sheikh Muhammad. The name Burj Al-Arab means 'Tower of the Arabs' in Arabic. The architecture is designed to look like the billowing sail of a traditional dhow, and at 321m (1,053ft) high, it is the world's second tallest hotel.

(Cont. on p82)

Beaches

One of the simplest and cheapest entertainments that Dubai has to offer is beachcombing, which can provide endless hours of distraction. The range of natural finds you may encounter is vast; the sandy beaches are themselves composed of millions of crushed shells from eons ago. The place to look is all along the high tide mark, especially after spring storms. High and low tide times are given in the local newspapers, along with sunrise and sunset times.

Public beaches

There are some public beaches in Dubai, as opposed to those privately owned by hotels, but on Fridays and holidays they are very heavily frequented and most Western expatriates prefer to join beach clubs. These are normally part of a hotel or resort, where you are guaranteed privacy and congenial surroundings as well as the convenience of showers and a bar. Most beach clubs have high joining fees and then an annual membership fee that varies according to the facilities.

The other more affordable options are the beach parks of Jumeirah and Al-Mamzar, which also have showers, changing facilities and lifeguards. Bikini beachwear for women, as long as both halves are worn, and swimming trunks for men are fine. Dogs are banned from the beaches, as is driving. The best undeveloped public beach is beyond Jebel Ali Golf Resort and Spa and the Palm Jebel Ali,

A public beach area near Dubai Marina

The private beach of a five-star hotel

where there is a 10km (6-mile) stretch of sand, but you need permission from Dubai Municipality if you want to camp or barbecue. Kitesurfers are frequently to be found on this stretch, driven off the other beaches by increasingly tight restrictions.

Sea dangers

The water looks calm and inviting, but you should be aware that there are occasional strong rip tides. Take care not to swim too far out from the shore, as even strong swimmers have sometimes found themselves swept out. The water itself can also harbour some dangerous creatures, although the threat from these should not be exaggerated as it is only slight.

Sea snakes, for example, are not naturally aggressive and, although they are very poisonous, the reality is that they cannot open their small mouths wide enough to get hold of anything bigger than a child's finger. You may sometimes find the snakes – which are yellow and black, measuring about 1–2m (3–6ft) long – washed up on the beach, waiting for the next tide to take them back to the sea; it's best just to leave them be. As for sharks, there are at least ten different species of these in the Arabian Gulf, but they rarely come close to the shore.

DOUBLED COASTLINE

The effect of the plan to build the trio of Palm Island developments just offshore (the Jumeirah, the Deira and the Jebel Ali) would be to double Dubai's 72km (45-mile) coastline, adding 4,000 beachfront lots for villas and apartments and disrupting the marine ecosystem. However, only the Jumeirah Palm is complete.

Standing on its own specially constructed island to add to its exclusivity, the Burj Al-Arab can only be approached via a guarded barrier, and you will need a reservation to dine there. If you are prepared to pay the sky-high prices, you can go for afternoon tea in the lobby lounge Sahn Eddar, or for cocktails at the Sky View Bar. The 'seven-star' hotel boasts 202 duplex suites, each with its own internal staircase, and the sheer extravagance of the internal décor can be a little overwhelming.

The Burj Al-Arab can only be accessed if you have made a reservation

A view of the huge port area at Jebel Ali

Work began in 1994, and the hotel's doors were opened to the first guests in 1999. At night, the Burj Al-Arab's exterior lights change colour, forming an unmistakable landmark.
Off Jumeirah Road. Tel: 301 7600. www.jumeirah.com

Jebel Ali

This is the world's largest man-made port and the United Arab Emirates' biggest Free Zone. The incentives for the zone are exemption from corporation tax for 15 years, no personal income tax, no currency restrictions, 100 per cent repatriation of capital and profits, superb communications, easy labour recruitment, and no import or export duties. In the United Arab Emirates as a whole, companies must be at least 51 per cent owned by nationals, but in the Jebel Ali Free Zone, 100 per cent foreign companies can be registered. Big names here include BP, Sony, Kodak, IBM and Acer computers.

Sheikh Rashid conceived the idea of the Free Zone in 1976 while on a camping trip in the Jebel Ali area. The story goes that he struck his walking stick into a dune and announced that the US$1,000 million industrial port would be constructed on that spot. The new airport at Jebel Ali, renamed Al Maktoum International Airport, opened its first runway in 2010 for cargo-only flights. When funds permit, it plans to have five runways and be ten times larger than Dubai International, becoming the largest airport in the world.

ADVANTAGES OF BEING A NATIONAL

The nationals of the United Arab Emirates are among the best looked after and most privileged of any in the world. In addition to free health care of the highest quality, heavily subsidised water and electricity, marriage grants, extra benefits for large numbers of children and generous pensions for older nationals, there are a number of privileges that enable them to earn money from trade agencies, or from renting property built with government-provided loans on freely distributed land. Nationals are also given priority in job allocations.

The Dubai Creek golf course has a very distinctive clubhouse

SPORTS FACILITIES

Golf courses

As with so many other sports, Dubai has carved out a niche for itself as the premier golf destination of the Gulf and Middle East, hosting the Dubai Desert Classic since the early 1990s at the magnificent Emirates Golf Club. With prize money of over US$2.2 million, this is one of the richest tournaments in the world, running for four days in late February or early March and naturally attracting the world's top players, such as Tiger Woods and Colin Montgomerie. **Dubai Golf** (*www.dubaigolf.com*) operates a central reservation system for anyone wanting to book a round of golf on any of the emirate's major courses.

Dubai Creek Golf and Yacht Club
This club has recently undergone a major redevelopment, both of the course itself and of the distinctive clubhouse. It has a floodlit driving range and extensive practice facilities. *Opposite the Deira City Centre Mall. Tel: 295 6000. www.dubaigolf.com*

Emirates Golf Club
The club offers two 18-hole championship courses, of which the par 72 Majlis course was the first grass course in the Middle East. The course is maintained at terrific cost with an immensely complex automatic watering system. It is mown three times a week and the greens are mown daily, and it is fed with a blend of fertilisers every three days. Before grass courses existed

in the Middle East, golfers had to walk around carrying a small patch of Astroturf to put down on the sand fairways for each stroke. The club also offers two driving ranges and dedicated practice areas.
Interchange No 5 off Sheikh Zayed Highway. Tel: 380 2222. www.dubaigolf.com

Ski Dubai

This extraordinary ski slope is a world within a world, a level of unreality that is extreme even by Dubai standards. Set behind massive walls of glass is the world's largest indoor snow park, its temperature permanently set at –5°C (23°F). It boasts five slopes to suit all levels, from gentle nursery slopes for beginners to the world's first indoor 'black run'. There are chairlifts and drag-lifts, and the attached shop sells everything you might need for the slopes.

Skiing is not compulsory as there is also a toboggan run, or you can even just throw snowballs and roll in the snow. Only competent skiers are allowed straight on the slopes; beginners can take lessons with qualified instructors. Any family members not interested in snowballing or skiing can simply watch through the glass from the après-ski log cabin cafés complete with log fires, or wander around the shops of the mall.
Mall of the Emirates. Tel: 409 8000; www.skidxb.com. Open: Sun–Wed 10am–11pm, Thur 10am–midnight, Fri 9am–midnight, Sat 9am–11pm. Admission charge with additional charges for a 2-hour ski pass including the hire of all kit except gloves.

The toboggan run at Ski Dubai

Theme parks

Dubai is heaven on earth if you like your entertainment packaged, and as you would expect, theme parks figure large here. As the city expands, so does the appetite for further amusement, and the list of parks is growing constantly.

Al-Nasr Leisureland

The oldest of Dubai's leisure parks, Al-Nasr may seem a little outdated now, but it is still popular for its huge ice-skating rink that is big enough for ice hockey, its bowling alley and its amusement park. Leisureland also has a fitness centre, two swimming pools (one for adults and one for children), a sauna and tennis courts; this part operates like a club with annual membership. The theme park is located in an area given over to schools, mosques and hospitals between Creekside Park and the Karama district.

Oud Metha. Tel: 337 1234. www.alnasrll.com. Open: 11am–9pm (summer); 11am–5pm (winter). Admission charge.

Fun for all the family at Global Village

Global Village

Global Village rises up from the sands like some mirage of a global theme park, offering a heady mix of rides, culture, shows, craft items and food from all over the world.

On its own site at the edge of the city off the Emirates Road. www.globalvillage.ae. Open: Nov–Mar Sat–Wed 4pm–midnight (families only on Mon), Thur–Fri 4pm–1am.

Wild Wadi Waterpark

Spread over 5ha (12 acres) between the Burj Al-Arab and Jumeirah Beach hotels, this world-class water park is themed around the adventures of

A waterfall in the Wild Wadi Waterpark

Juha, the legendary friend of Sinbad the Sailor. There are 23 aquatic rides, and there are usually queues for the more popular ones.

It is best to make a day of it, as the one-off admission charge is high, but the ticket does cover unlimited rides once you are in. There are two cafés serving drinks and snacks.

The rides vary in fright degrees from the gentle Juha's Journey, where you just sit back and float in double or single rubber rings through the changing landscape, to the terrifying Jumeirah Sceirah, the fastest and tallest free-fall water slide outside North America. Another unusual attraction is the Wipeout, a permanently rolling wave where you can show off your bodyboarding talents.

The entrance is right beside the approach to the Burj Al-Arab Hotel. Tel: 348 4444. www.wildwadi.com. Open: Nov–Feb 10am–6pm; Mar–May & Sept–Oct 10am– 7pm; June–Aug 10am–9pm. Admission charge covers unlimited rides.

Wonderland

This 13ha (32-acre) fun park opened in 1997. It cost Dh120 million to build and currently offers 30 attractions including roller-coasters, go-carts, paintballing, trampolines, and video and arcade games. The water park section is called Splashland and has a relatively high one-off charge for its nine rides, which include slides and twisters, a lazy river, bridges and water cannons. Like Al-Nasr Leisureland, it also has an adult pool and a children's activity pool with slides, so you can just relax there while older children explore the rides. The businessman behind the scheme, Ali Albwardy, has completed many other ventures, and in fact runs Dubai's luxurious Polo Club as a hobby. Many of Wonderland's managers were poached from the UK's Alton Towers.

Between the Garhoud Bridge and the Wafi Mall. Tel: 324 1222. Open: 11am–9pm (summer); 11am–5pm (winter). Admission charge covers rides.

Dubai: beyond the city

Dubai is the most centrally located of the emirates and has the best road connections. Therefore, if you are prepared to make early starts and do not mind drives of two to three hours each way, most of the places described in this section are a day trip from Dubai city.

Most visitors to Dubai are surprised to discover how much the emirate has to offer beyond the city's obvious attractions of shopping malls, souks, sport and beaches. As you head inland away from the coast, the landscape begins to change, and even the sand dunes present themselves in a remarkable variety of guises. After about an hour's drive, the dramatic outline of the Hajar mountains rises up on the horizon, concealing remote wadis, hidden oases and cool pools, a side of Dubai that often remains

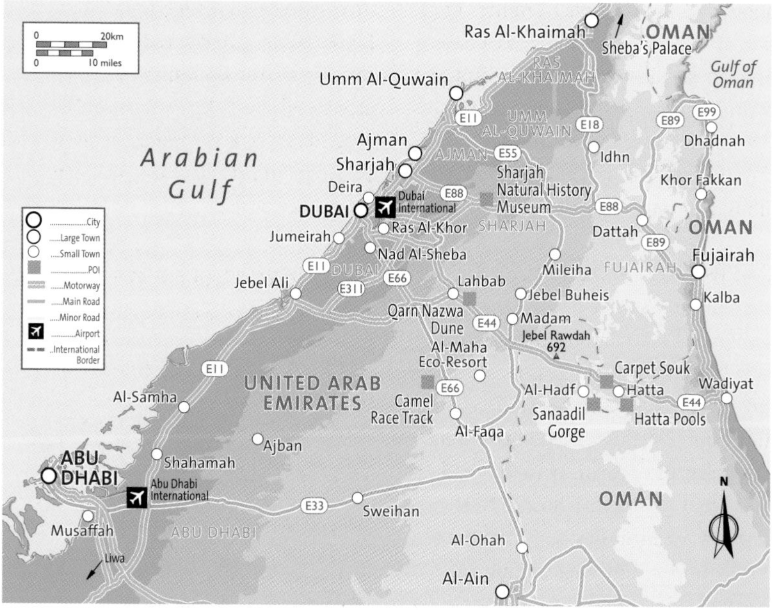

The roads beyond the city are usually almost free of traffic

unexplored. At weekends especially, it can be a welcome break to escape the city and seek out a little nature.

Hatta, Dubai's mountain enclave about one hour's drive from the city, is a good destination to use as a base. The signs to Hatta are clearly displayed from Interchange No 1 off the Sheikh Zayed Highway, and subsequently at the succession of roundabouts found along the road as it exits the city.

QARN NAZWA DUNE (BIG RED)

Half an hour's drive beyond the city on the E44 Hatta road, you cannot help but notice the huge dune to the left of the road, Qarn Nazwa Dune, affectionately nicknamed Big Red. Its sheer size and proximity to the road mean that it attracts a host of four-wheel drive enthusiasts, keen to try out their desert driving techniques (*see pp92–3*). Tour operators offer sandboarding and sand-skiing trips where you can slide down the dune as if on a snowboard, and then get driven back to the top by four-wheel drive as your chairlift equivalent. Locals and expatriate residents come in their own four-wheel drives and use either locally sold sandboards or even plastic sledges or trays. On Fridays, the slopes can get very crowded.

THE ROMANCE OF SAND

The redness of the sand is explained by the presence of iron oxide, a feature of the arid climate. There are numerous types of sand, classed according to the shape and fineness of the grains. Abu Dhabi sand is mostly rounded, whereas the best building sand is angular for greater strength. The whole Arabian Peninsula has rather coarse grains, but glass, for example, needs fine grains. Absurdly, Saudi Arabia imports sand from Finland for glass manufacture.

AL-HADF AND THE SANAADIL GORGE

This day trip or half-day trip from Dubai city does not require four-wheel drive and is about the easiest and quickest of any excursion to the mountains. The trip is an excellent introduction to gentle off-road driving, with striking scenery, the gorge and rock pools. The trip can be as short as three hours: one hour for the drive itself each way, and one hour for walking in the gorge, and only one car is needed (*see pp94–5*). Alternatively, it can be extended to a whole day by taking a picnic and exploring the wadi beyond, which has a few ruins and more rock pools. You are unlikely to encounter anyone beyond some Beluch and Pakistanis tending the cultivated date gardens in the villages. Al-Hadf and Sanaadil both lie in Omani territory, in the bulge that can be entered from the United Arab Emirates without a visa. You will re-enter the United Arab Emirates shortly before the Hatta enclave.

Having entered Oman, where the signpost announces 'Welcome', and arrived at the first mountains shortly

THE MATING OF PALM TREES

There are male and female date palms, and the farmer carries out pollination by cutting off flowering branches of the male tree, climbing the female tree and placing the male branches among the female branches. This process is repeated two or three times to make sure it is successful. In Arabic, there are over 500 different words to describe the date in its various types and conditions, which illustrates the measure of its importance.

A traditional rest area in Al-Hadf

The distinctive black volcanic mountains in Dubai's interior

after the Madam roundabout, the signpost off to Al-Hadf 6km (3¾ miles) is marked to the right just a few kilometres later. The road is tarmacked now, and you follow it for about 4km (2½ miles) until you reach the edge of the small village of Sanaadil. Turn right, skirting the village, and within 1km (⅔ mile) you will come to a date palm grove on your right, with the beginnings of the gorge down below to your left. In a car, you may have to stop at any point here, but in a four-wheel drive vehicle, you can drive on a further 1km (⅔ mile) to where the bumpy track flattens out beside a wadi bed, and park the car. From here, you can retrace your tracks on foot into the wadi bed itself, passing rock pools as the gorge narrows and deepens. Where it gets too narrow to continue, clamber up and follow the gorge from the top. At certain times of year, the gorge culminates in a large lake-sized pool where you can easily swim.

If you return to the car and walk off in the opposite direction further into the mountains, you will find some curious stone foundations of old settlements on a few of the lower hills. The mountainous landscapes are very attractive, with a surprising amount of vegetation, but make sure you are well protected from the sun with sun hat and suncream if you are out and about in the middle of the day.

Off-road driving techniques

The cardinal rules for driving in soft sand are as follows:

1 Stick to a steady speed in second or third gear. Always try to drive gently and sympathetically.

2 Try not to change gear unless it is essential.

3 Turn the steering wheel gently from side to side as you drive, to help stay on the crest of the sand.

4 Carry four pieces of carpet, one to put under each wheel, in case you get stuck. The most convenient way is to keep the carpet in the footwell of each seat.

5 Deflate tyres to 20psi (1.38 bar) or a little lower if you get stuck, to improve your grip.

6 Travel with another vehicle, unless you are very experienced and know the route well.

7 Always carry a tow rope and a shovel.

Several organisations offer desert driving courses with instruction by professional drivers. These are run regularly at weekends for residents, and some are for women only. The four-wheel-drive vehicles are provided on some courses, but it is cheaper to receive instruction using your own vehicle.

For four-wheel driving in wet wadis, which is quite different to sand driving, the following advice applies:

1 The maximum safe depth is to the tops of the tyres.

2 Cross where the water is at its widest as this tends to be where it is shallowest and has the least strong current.

Drive into the wilderness to see a dramatic desert sunrise

Many Dubaians own a 4WD vehicle

3 Keep your speed down if the water is fairly shallow so you do not splash your electrics.
4 With deeper water, enter slowly in four-wheel-drive low gear (first or second). Keep the revs high once the front grill is in the water to create a slight bow wave with a trough under the engine. Charging at water full speed is unnecessary and may cause flooding of the engine.
5 If your engine does get waterlogged, do not attempt to start it as water may have entered the tops of the pistons via the exhaust or air filter. Ask for help towing the vehicle out of the water, remove and dry the spark plugs, dry the ignition system, then turn on the ignition to pump the water out of the combustion chamber. Once the water is out, you can reassemble the spark plugs and leads (taking care to get them in the right order), then try the ignition or push start the vehicle if your battery is low.

Careful planning is required before any trip off-road. The best months to go are mid-October to mid-May before the weather becomes too hot to be bearable. Make sure your vehicle is in perfect condition, with all the levels checked and the tyre pressures at the correct settings. You must take enough water – at least 4 litres (7 pints) of water per person per day. This is absolutely vital. For food, the important thing is to take items that do not go off, for example, dried and tinned food, and citrus fruit that are simple and easy to prepare. Always take an emergency supply of dates – one pack per person will give you peace of mind and mean that you can survive many days of deprivation.

Drive: Hatta

Dubai's mountain enclave of Hatta lies about 100km (62 miles) from Dubai city, and 10km (6 miles) from the Dubai–Oman border. This is an excellent escape from the city, and you can camp overnight in a wadi, stay at the luxurious Hatta Fort Hotel or simply return to the city.

The drive is 105km (65 miles) and takes just over an hour, depending on your cruising speed, on a good and easy road that empties quite quickly once you are clear of the city.

From Interchange No 1, Sheikh Zayed Highway (the main roundabout from which Hatta is signposted, along with Oman), follow the Hatta signs as the road passes through the Nad Al-Sheba area of the city to reach the Bukadra interchange, where five roads meet. Take care at this point to follow the Hatta sign, rather than the one for Al-Ain, leaving the Rugby Club on your right. The road is Ras Al-Khor.

1 Ras Al-Khor

The road here is called Ras Al-Khor because it skirts the bottom end of the Creek. To your left you will see the Ras

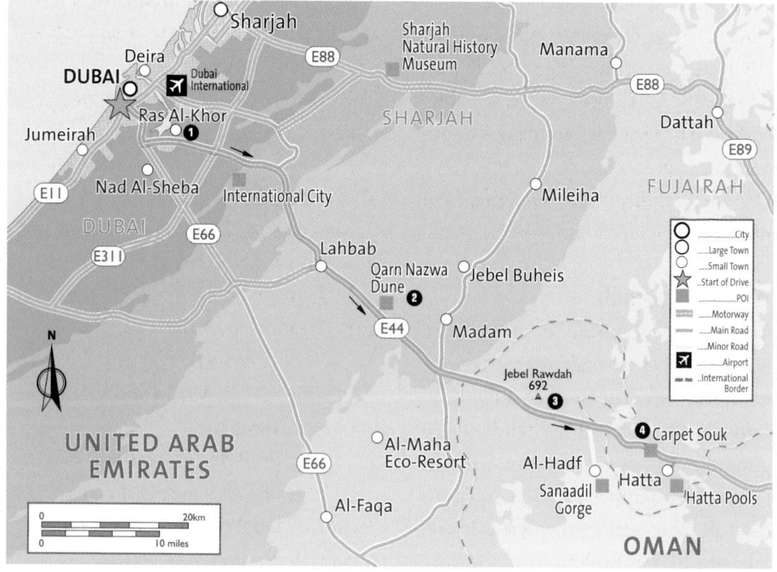

Al-Khor Wildlife Sanctuary and Flamingo Island, and you may even be lucky enough to spot some flamingos. To your right is a heavily industrialised area, generally packed with trucks, which you will be glad to escape.

At the next series of roundabouts, follow the Hatta/Oman signs, passing International City on your right, until you leave the built-up area behind you. Half an hour further, 15km (9 miles) beyond the Lahbab roundabout, the dunes start to become red and there is a dramatic outcrop by a petrol station on the left, with a further outcrop to the right. Shortly after, a break in the fence reveals the Qarn Nazwa Dune, nicknamed Big Red, rising up on your left.

Qarn Nazwa Dune is also popular with sandboarders

2 Qarn Nazwa Dune

The Qarn Nazwa Dune, or Big Red, is favoured by four-wheel-drive enthusiasts as the closest place to the city to test desert driving skills. If you don't want to take part, watching the enthusiasts perform can make a good spectator sport.

Continue southeast for another half hour towards the mountains.

3 Jebel Rawdah

The impressive mountain that you first come to, Jebel Rawdah, with greenish deposits to the left (immediately opposite the turn-off to Mahdah), is a good place for fossil-hunting. You can turn off onto any number of tracks to have a picnic under an acacia tree and try your luck at finding a marine life fossil as all these mountains were once on the seabed until a volcanic eruption thrust them upwards.

As you keep driving, you enter the outskirts of Hatta.

4 Carpet Souk

Lining both sides of the road there are rows and rows of carpet stalls, displaying an array of wares, and a few other craft items. This is a good place to pick up a new rug and practise your bargaining skills. Most carpets are new and very colourful.

Continue until the roundabout in front of the Hatta Fort Hotel, and take the road to the right uphill towards the Hatta Heritage Village (see p96)*.*

Learn about Dubai's traditions at the Heritage Village

HATTA HERITAGE VILLAGE AND ENVIRONS

Hatta Heritage Village

The village is set between two hills crowned by watchtowers in the centre of new Hatta town. Completed in 1996, it recreates the old village that had fallen into disuse. The original settlement here is thought to date back to the 16th century. Apart from the buildings themselves, probably the most charming aspect of the place is the restored *falaj* (irrigation) system, which has a fine, strong flow. There are several places where access has been made easy by steps. The mosque has been dated to 1850, and in the centre of the village stands the fort, the oldest in the emirate, a strong and simple structure built in 1790 around a courtyard, now used to display weaponry. There are some 30 houses of various sizes and types, all true to the original patterns. Several houses are built right into the hillside and are made of *barasti* (palm frond), while others belonging to wealthier owners are built of mountain stones and mud.

Tombs

The green wire fence guards a circular tomb that measures 8m (26ft) across and is divided into chambers. If you continue on the track, you will come to several more fenced tombs on the hillside. All of these are in what is known as the Umm Al-Nar style, after those found in Abu Dhabi, and date to *c.* 2700 BC. This culture is known to have had links to the Sumerian culture of Mesopotamia.

Follow the road beyond the Heritage Village for 0.6km (1/3 mile) to reach a junction with a white mosque. Turn left here and follow the road for a further 0.9km (1/2 mile) until you come to a junction with a tarmac road forking right at right angles. Follow the right fork, with its many speed humps, for 3.4km (2 miles) and then take the track to the left that leads between two farms. Follow the track for 0.9km (1/2 mile) until you reach another fork, where you take the right fork down into a rocky wadi and continue up the other side.

Hatta pools

There is very little vegetation and therefore very little shade in the area of the pools, so it is best to explore at either end of the day. Try to avoid Fridays because the sheer volume of 4WD vehicles, pick-up trucks and cars is depressing, and many of them come complete with blaring transistor radios and attendant litter. The best way to explore the area is on foot, and you can follow the course of the wadi northwards to discover gorge-like rock formations, with pools and waterfalls.

From the tombs, return to the tarmac road, and now turn left and continue a further 6km (3 3/4 miles) to where the tarmac ends. Here, the well-graded track forks right (south) into the mountains, running like a roller-coaster up and down an endless series of hills. After three turn-offs which you can ignore, the track opens out into Wadi Qahfi – approximately 6km (3 3/4 miles) from the end of the tarmac road. After a long, steep descent, look out for the first track to the left, which descends into the wadi and down to a rough parking area above the pools.

The dramatic mountain range above the Heritage Village at Hatta

Camels are muzzled if they are considered bad-tempered

MIDMAAR SIBAAQ AL-HUJUN (CAMEL RACE TRACK)

The Camel Race Track is one of Dubai's major attractions, but it must be visited in the early morning to see it at its best. Actual races take place during the winter months between 7.30 and 8.30am, but the camels are taken out every morning at this time to be exercised, irrespective of the races. The photo opportunities are endless, as camels pour out from their pens, crossing the road and bringing all the traffic to a halt.

Each owner has a different set of colours, so all their camels are immediately recognisable from a distance, and with the multicoloured camel blankets, halters and lead ropes, the whole spectacle makes for very colourful viewing.

Camel racing is serious business. The price of a racing camel starts at around £40,000 and champion thoroughbreds can fetch over £1.5 million. The average length of the race is 13km (8 miles) and the winner usually gets a prestige car or a four-

CHILD JOCKEYS

Much bad publicity was recently generated over the child jockeys often used in camel racing, who are sometimes as young as three or four. Most were shipped across from the subcontinent, sold by their parents, but international pressure about human rights violations has now made this illegal. In their place, new robotic jockeys have been invented, operated by remote control from their owners' 4WD vehicles as they follow the track, again something uniquely Dubaian.

wheel drive. Owners follow the race alongside the track in their own 4WD vehicles, yelling encouragement. The races on National Day and at the religious festivals are the most important of the year (*see pp18–19*).

A short way from the track, look out for the camel market, a group of simple single-storey huts arranged in a square. There is an assortment of shops selling every kind of camel accessory imaginable, along with the feed. The camel blankets can be fun used as picnic rugs or even bedspreads.

The camel race track has recently been moved to a new location 50km (31 miles) south of the city, off the Al-Ain road. It is well-signposted. Open: daily; races are run Oct–Mar Thur & Fri 7.30–8.30am. Free admission.

Early-morning competitors preparing on the race track

Day trips to neighbouring emirates

Dubai receives so much media attention and appears so dominant in all fields that it is often mistaken for the capital of the United Arab Emirates, in the same way that Istanbul and Sydney are frequently mistaken as national capitals. Abu Dhabi is in fact the capital, and the largest by far of the seven emirates in terms of area, though Dubai is the largest city.

The formal boundaries between the emirates were only settled in 1979. During this elaborate process, made necessary by the discovery of oil, two Arabic-speaking British diplomats travelled by camel from one settlement to another questioning the village headman, and establishing

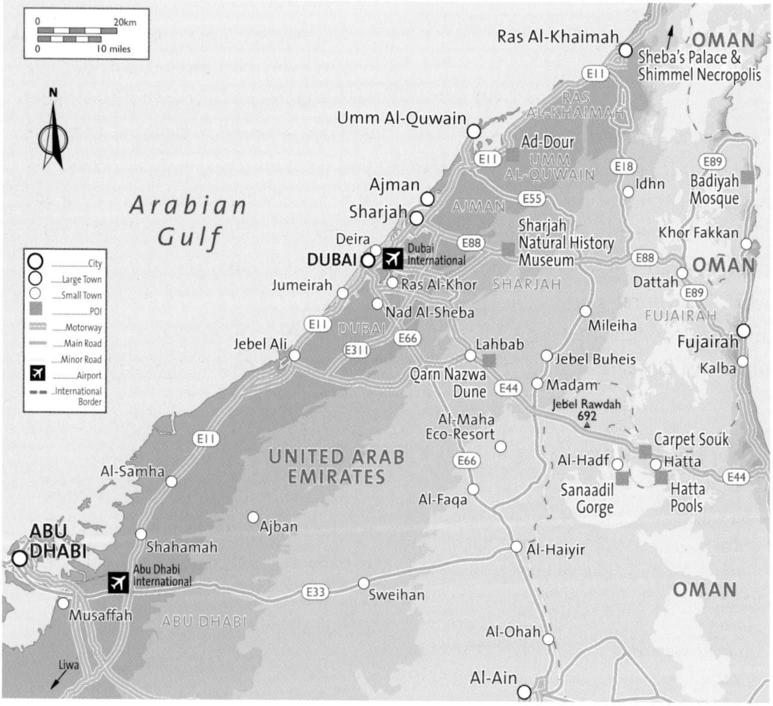

Abu Dhabi is the capital of the United Arab Emirates

which sheikh the village owed its allegiance to.

Each of the seven emirates is changing so quickly, and its relationships with the other six developing constantly, that it is hard to keep track. The character of each Emirati ruler has an enormous bearing on the character of the emirate, rather like a school and its head teacher, but the remarkable thing is the extent to which the emirates have held together and withstood the pressures and strains of the last 30 years. A political and religious tolerance has evolved that has become a hallmark of the way the United Arab Emirates is viewed in the outside world. It has enabled this small country to play a role far greater than its size merits as a voice of conciliation and compromise in regional and Arab politics. This has not always been easy at times of potential conflict, such as during the Iran–Iraq war (1980–88) or during Operation Desert Shield (1990–91); when there are mixed feelings about the extent of American involvement in the region; or over potentially thorny issues, like shared water resources and electricity, within the Gulf Cooperation Council.

Across the United Arab Emirates, 85 per cent of the population is expatriate, 15 per cent national, and in Dubai expatriates outnumber nationals by about six to one.

After Dubai, Sharjah and Ras Al-Khaimah are the two emirates

THE SEVEN EMIRATES BY SIZE

Abu Dhabi	64,750sq km/24,994sq miles
Dubai	3,900sq km/1,506sq miles
Sharjah	2,600sq km/1,004sq miles
Ras Al-Khaimah	1,690sq km/653sq miles
Fujairah	1,170sq km/452sq miles
Umm Al-Quwain	780sq km/301sq miles
Ajman	260sq km/100sq miles

Sharjah University, cornerstone of the UAE's education system

that have most to offer the visitor; Sharjah because of its museums, Ras Al-Khaimah because of its attractive mountain scenery and interesting archaeological sites. The beaches and diving at Fujairah are distinct attractions, while both Umm Al-Quwain and Ajman, the poorest and smallest of the emirates, have their own sleepy charm, and some fine forts. The following pages describe the places easily visited from Dubai in a day, although some, like the trips to Al-Ain and Abu Dhabi, would be better with an overnight stay.

SHARJAH: CULTURAL CAPITAL

Education

'Enough of concrete, let us build the human being.' This has been the constant slogan of the ruler of Sharjah, Dr Sheikh Sultan Bin Muhammad Al-Qasimi, who holds PhDs from two British universities. Since he became ruler in 1972, he has set out to make Sharjah a cultural centre, and in 1998 his efforts were rewarded when it won the title of 'Cultural Capital of the Arab World'. His wife, too, must take much of the credit for initiating many facilities for women, such as the Sharjah Women's Club – in pride of place beside the Ruler's Palace. The first girls' school was opened here, and in the late 1960s Sharjah was the only emirate to have a girls' secondary school. Education remains a priority for Sharjah, and even its TV station produces many of its own programmes with an educational or cultural content.

No alcohol

There are signs today that Sharjah's anti-alcohol policy – it is the only 'dry' emirate – is damaging its economic future, as tourists and businesses flock instead to the more liberal culture of neighbouring Dubai, despite its higher prices. In pre-oil days, Sharjah was the most prosperous and dominant of the emirates – a bustling trading port with its Creek the headquarters of the great Qawasim seafaring tribe – while Abu Dhabi was just a simple fishing village and Dubai a modest trading town on its Creek. Inland too, Sharjah had the fertile area around Dhaid where much fruit and vegetable produce could be grown to supply Sharjah town.

British links

In the first half of the 20th century, Sharjah was the headquarters of the British-sponsored Trucial Oman Scouts, and it was home to a Royal Air Force base and a residence for the British political agent. It therefore had more of a British presence than any other emirate. This was because in the 1930s the ruler had offered the British the right to build a landing strip and airport, the United Arab Emirates' first, whereas the rulers of Abu Dhabi, Dubai and Ras Al-Khaimah had all refused. This brought Sharjah valuable extra income at a time when the pearling industry had virtually ceased because of the advent of Japanese cultured pearls.

A mosque in Sharjah, on the road to Ajman

Modest oil reserves

In the 1970s, oil was discovered here in commercial quantities, and Sharjah still produces a modest amount. It has three enclaves over on the east coast – Dibba, Khor Fakkan and Kalba – all of which are also 'dry'.

Sharjah vistas

The approach to Sharjah from Dubai is hardly prepossessing. You appear simply to be swapping one set of modern buildings and skyscrapers for another, except that Sharjah's buildings appear less affluent and the streets are narrower. There is also an apparently endless industrial hinterland as Sharjah is in fact the most industrialised of any of the emirates, with well over 600 small to medium-sized companies attracted by business incentives from the authorities. Sharjah Airport, in support of these industries, is a very busy cargo centre.

Sharjah has a corniche with a few beach hotels – all 'dry' – and its Creek has been landscaped, with gardens running all around the edge and a dramatic 100m (328ft)-high fountain, making it a popular stroll for local families in the evenings.

Persian carpets

Sharjah is reputed to be the cheapest place in the Gulf to buy carpets, and shopping is made easy by the wealth of souks, all of them easily accessible by car and with an abundance of parking, unlike Dubai where parking in the souk areas is a serious challenge. The upstairs areas of the blue-tiled Souk Al-Markazi (Central Souk/New Souk) are some of the best, with alley-like corridors selling antiques, traditional jewellery and a huge quantity of carpets which have come over in dhows from Iran.

Sharjah is the best place to buy bargain rugs

The cardinal rule when buying something like a carpet is to never show interest in the one you really like. Make sure your voice expresses dissatisfaction and always convey that it is not really quite what you are looking for. That way, your bargaining technique will be at its most effective. Never buy in a hurry, and ask the carpet dealer as many questions as you can think of, for example, the symbols used and their meanings, to help increase your knowledge for future purchases. It makes a big difference if you understand something about what you are buying. Here are some tips to folllow before buying:

- Look at the closeness of the weave: the closer the weave and the smaller the knots on the back, the better the quality and durability of the carpet. Nine hundred knots is top of the range.
- Check for artificial colouring by rubbing a damp handkerchief over a corner of the carpet.
- Part the weave and see if the colour at the base is the same as on top. Some dealers will age a carpet by leaving it out in the sun to fade. Some rugs are artificially aged by washing in bleach, a

A traditional souk in Sharjah

process that rots the fibres and reduces the carpet's life. A quick sniff usually reveals whether bleach has been used.

- Always check the reverse side of the carpet for signs of damage and moth infestation, apparent from small white sticky smears in the weave.

Most of the carpets on sale in the emirates are new or almost new. The dealer will always tell you that this is their special price just for you, but no matter what they say, you will only be getting a good deal if you knock at least a third off the original asking price.

NATURAL AND CHEMICAL DYES

Traditionally, natural dyes were used to colour wool, cotton and silk. These dyes were derived – often by lengthy and laborious processes – from roots, bark, berries, vegetables and minerals. In the second half of the 19th century, aniline chemical dyes became available, and these have gradually replaced most of the old vegetable dyes. Watch out for pink and orange in rugs that are claiming to be older than this, as these are colours that could never be produced from natural dyes. The quality of chemical dyes has now improved considerably, and they can be quite deceptive. If you want to be convinced that colours are natural, look out for mid-weave colour changes, because with natural dyes there are always slight variations of colour between batches.

Walk: Old Sharjah

With the advent of oil money in the 1970s, many of the old buildings throughout the emirates were replaced with concrete high rises. By the 1980s, little remained of the traditional architecture, but Sharjah was the first to realise the importance of preserving what remained. As a result, no other emirate has such finely restored authentic buildings.

Allow 3 hours for the walk, including the visiting time. The total distance is around 2km (1¼ miles).

Approach from Sharjah Creek (Khor Khalid), following the road past the Fish and Plant Souks towards the dhow corniche, then turn right off the first roundabout on the corniche, to enter a wide street lined with banks and straddled by the old fort. Turn right just before reaching the fort, to find the Naboodah House about 200m (220yds) further on.

1 Naboodah House

This late 19th-century two-storey house built from coral stone belonged to the wealthy merchant Al-Naboodah in the early 20th century. It was the first to be restored and now doubles as Sharjah's Heritage Museum. The splendour and relative luxury of this house is remarkable, and each of the 20 or so rooms has been carefully recreated with period furnishings and décor.
Open: Tue–Thur, Sat & Sun 9am–1pm & 5–8pm (Wed: women only), Fri 4.30–8.30pm. Closed: Mon.
Free admission.

Cross the courtyard with its traditional-style swings and see-saws to enter the souk opposite.

2 Souk Al-Arsah

This traditional souk has been completely renovated. Now roofed and air-conditioned, the stone-built stalls, some 100 in all, have wooden shutters. This is the perfect place for souvenir shopping, with antiques, bric-a-brac, jewellery, musical instruments and even model dhows all displayed in clean and shaded lanes.

In the same restored complex, walk over to the Islamic Museum, formerly Bait Saeed Bin Muhammad Al-Shamsi.

3 Islamic Museum

Extremely smart with automatic glass doors, this large merchant's house has been spaciously laid out. Its air-conditioned corridors display an impressive collection of illuminated Korans, pottery and tiles from Iran, Afghanistan, Turkey and Syria, and even an astrolabe, an early navigation device.

Open: Tue–Thur, Sat & Sun 9am–1pm & 5–8pm (Wed: women only), Fri 9am–1pm & 4.30–8.30pm. Closed: Mon. Admission charge.

Now walk northeast (right), parallel to the sea, to reach the big main road, Bank St, where the old fort sits to your right.

Collections of memorabilia in Sharjah's Artists' Quarter

4 Al-Husn (Old Ruler's fort)

Originally built in 1822 and demolished in 1969, all that remained of this, the most impressive fort in all the emirates, was one tower. All four towers have now been restored, using old photos for guidance. This was a massive project completed in 1997 under the personal supervision of the ruler. Inside, there are many fine old photos, and an old cinema reel shows footage of the first planes landing here from London in the 1930s.

Walk 400m (440yds) further northeast to reach the Artists' Quarter.

5 Artists' Quarter

This is a whole area of renovated buildings comprising an Artists' Souk, an Arts Café, the Sharjah Art Galleries with artists' studios, and the massive three-storey **Art Museum**, the biggest by far of its kind in the Gulf. You could easily spend several hours here alone.

Art Museum. Open: Sat–Thur 8am–8pm, Fri 4–8pm.

Yachts on Sharjah Creek

Sharjah's museums

Sharjah has more museums than any other emirate, a fact it is very proud of. The new ones tend to be concentrated around the Culture roundabout, also known as Book roundabout, with a model of an open Koran as its centrepiece.

Sharjah Archaeology Museum

This swish museum was designed as an attractive blend of traditional Islamic and Arab architecture. It opened in 1997, with parking for 300 cars, a spacious cafeteria and a corridor linking it to the Science Museum.

The museum is arranged chronologically and on entering the 'Gateway to the Past', you start with the oldest phase of 5000–3000 BC, in which huge film screens explain (in Arabic and English) how early humans here were hunter-gatherers. Next came the settled phase of farmers, traders and craftspeople, 3000–1000 BC, who learned to cultivate and irrigate crops. The oasis dwellers from 1300–300 BC were able for the first time to build *falaj* systems – underground tunnels bringing water from the mountains. The last section covers 300 BC–AD 600 and is dominated by a wealth of finds from Maleihah, Sharjah's most extensive archaeological site, with its tall tower tombs.

Sharjah city, just before the Science Museum on the way to Culture roundabout. Tel: (06) 566 5466. www.sharjahmuseums.ae. Open: Mon–Thur & Sat 9am–1pm & 5–8pm, Fri 5–8pm. Closed: Sun. Admission charge.

KORANIC QUOTE

Assuredly the creation
Of the heavens
And the earth
Is a greater matter
Than the creation of man:
Yet most men
Understand not.

Sura 40, Verse 57

Sharjah Natural History & Botanical Museum and Desert Park

This incredibly ambitious museum, which is now fully open again after renovation, tackles no less a subject than creation itself, using high-tech displays to the full, and bombarding all the senses. The history of the Earth, from Sharjah's point of view, is brilliantly explained, and you should not limit your time here. There is an extremely pleasant café, serving snacks and excellent cakes, and for company you can look out through a plate glass window at a pair of Arabian wolves. The Desert Park is a breeding centre for leopards, foxes, cheetahs, ibex, oryx and gazelles. Children are encouraged to feed and stroke the camels, horses, donkeys, geese, ducks and guinea fowl. If you have time to visit only one museum in the emirates, this should be it.

A 30-minute drive out of Sharjah at Junction 8 of the Sharjah–Dhaid Road. Tel: (06) 531 1411. www.sharjahmuseums.ae. Open: Sun, Mon, Wed & Thur 9am–5.30pm; Fri 2–5.30pm; Sat 11am–5.30pm. Closed: Tue. Admission charge.

The obelisk marks Sharjah's Desert Park

Sharjah Science Museum

Unique in the emirates, this museum, established in 1996, is set in landscaped grounds with ample parking. There are even stone-slab benches and tables for picnics. Inside, there is a café and snack bar, a good shop and clean toilets. The interior is extremely plush and beautifully laid out, with no expense spared. The exhibits are almost all interactive and are designed to illustrate scientific properties like sound and light, colour and gravity. In addition to the permanent exhibition halls, there is a planetarium, and showings of films in the auditorium at fixed times. These include subjects like the Internet and the digestive system. Children are well catered for.

Sharjah city, next to the television station beside Culture roundabout. Tel: (06) 566 8777. www.sharjahmuseums.ae. Open: Sun–Thur 8am–2pm, Fri & Sat 4–8pm. Admission charge; free for children under 3.

AJMAN

The smallest of the seven emirates, Ajman is less affluent than its neighbour Sharjah, to which it appears at first glance to be a mere extension. The trained eye, however, will detect little signs – the houses are less well finished and the streets are not so well provided with street lighting. Fishing from its own small creek and building dhows are Ajman's mainstays.

Corniche

As you pass through Sharjah along the corniche and out beyond the Ruler's Palace and the Sharjah Women's Club, with their beautifully landscaped roundabouts and avenues, you come to the roundabout at the Coral Beach Hotel. Beyond this is the border with Ajman, and so the next corniche is Ajman's. It is poorer and has fewer facilities than Sharjah's, although the Ajman Beach Hotel at the far end has now been taken over by the affluent Kempinski hotel chain.

Ajman fort/museum

This very well-laid-out fort/museum is set a little inland, and is Ajman's main attraction. The restoration has been sympathetic, retaining the fort's authentic feel. The outer courtyard is quite charming with its display of dhows and other boats, along with beautifully constructed replicas of traditional winter and summer houses from the pre-oil era. Just to the right of

The fort at Ajman is now a fascinating museum

the entrance gate, there is a reconstruction of a pair of 5,000-year-old tombs. At sunset, sitting in the simple courtyard cafeteria with the dusk calls to prayer ringing around the town and the museum staff kneeling to prayer on the grass, you can experience that rare feeling, if only for a moment, of being surrounded by natural indigenous culture.

The downstairs archaeology rooms display surprisingly rich finds from the two tombs, with delicate carnelian necklaces and pots sporting the black wavy lines characteristic of the Umm Al-Nar period. That some of these are still in one piece after 5,000 years is truly remarkable.

The display rooms upstairs are a delight to explore, with little staircases and a tiny series of rooms furnished as authentically as possible with coarse string matting and old carved chests. The weapons display is very impressive, and among the more unusual exhibits are traditional games, showing just how inventive children could be in the days before plastic toys and computers. The police exhibition is unusual, with its gas tear bombs and grisly photos of an execution carried out by firing squad. The fort doubled as the police headquarters until fairly recently.

Another rather gory section is the large exhibit hall of traditional medicine, showing what extraordinary techniques the people resorted to in the days before drugs and hospitals. The traditional wedding room displays costumes and explains that, until the 1950s, girls married from 12 onwards and boys from 17 onwards. The pearling and fishing displays are extremely well done with charming models of the boats and divers from the late 19th and early 20th centuries. On average, each diver collected ten oysters per dive. Finally, no one can visit this museum without coming away with an enhanced awareness of the importance of the palm tree.

Best reached from the corniche. Open: Sun–Thur 9am–noon & 5–8pm, Fri 5–8pm. Closed: Sat. Admission charge.

Ajman's best hotel, the Kempinski

There is very little traffic on the Umm Al-Quwain peninsula

UMM AL-QUWAIN

Probably the simplest and most unassuming of the seven emirates, Umm Al-Quwain, lying halfway between Dubai and Ras Al-Khaimah, can be a welcome breath of fresh air if you are looking for a change from commercialism, traffic and high-rise development.

Sometimes unkindly referred to as a windswept backwater, this is actually Umm Al-Quwain's attraction. In summer, its thin peninsula jutting out into the Gulf always catches the breeze, and the main road between Sharjah and Ras Al-Khaimah bypasses it, thereby ensuring peaceful and traffic-free roads. With its many offshore islands and lagoon, it has some of the best sailing in the United Arab Emirates.

As the second-smallest emirate after Ajman, Umm Al-Quwain has never had any significant industry except for fishing and shipbuilding. The dhow yards are still some of the most active in the United Arab Emirates, and this emirate's very name means 'Mother of the Two Powers', a reference to its long seafaring background. Early in the 20th century, Umm Al-Quwain was building about 20 dhows a year compared to Dubai's 10.

From Dubai, the drive takes 1 hour in normal traffic conditions.

Dreamland Aqua Park

Claiming to be the largest water park in the world, this fun park is conspicuous with its huge white dinosaur teeth fencing. It sells itself as being a mere 30-minute drive from Dubai, and offers, among other things, over 25 water rides, including a series of interconnecting tunnels to shoot through for those who love to terrify themselves.

Beside the main Sharjah–Ras Al-Khaimah Highway. Tel: (06) 768 1888.

www.dreamlanduae.com. Open: Jan–Mar & Sept–Dec 10am–6pm; Apr–June 10am–7pm (until 8pm June Thur–Sat); July–Aug 11am–9pm; Ramadan 10am–4pm. Admission charge; free for children under 3. Free transport system.

Aquarium

Unique in the United Arab Emirates, this aquarium is part of the Marine Research Centre of Umm Al-Quwain's Ministry of Agriculture and Fisheries. Inside, there are about 20 large tanks of live fish, all labelled with information on whether the fish is good to eat – useful for your next visit to the fish souk. There are also green turtles, whip-tailed rays and even the odd black-tipped reef shark. Of the stuffed displays, the huge swordfish and ray are the most impressive.

Situated on the headland beside the New Port. Open: Sat–Wed 8am–1pm, Thur 8–11am. Closed: Fri.

Old fort/museum

Umm Al-Quwain's picturesque old fort served as the town's police station until very recently. The most attractive room by far is the upstairs *majlis* (reception room) with its carved wooden verandas and high ceilings. The upstairs bathroom complexes are quite luxurious, with the floors sloping away to the drainage holes, more carefully designed than the average modern house. Since extensive restoration, the fort has been transformed into the emirate's museum, displaying treasures from the local archaeological sites of Ad-Dour and Tell Abraq.

In the heart of the Old Town. Open: Sun–Fri 10am–6pm. Closed: Sat.

Sinaiyyah Island

Directly opposite the main town lies this very flat barrier island that is now a nature reserve, home to the world's largest breeding colony of Socotra cormorants. A group of gazelles has also been introduced. The lagoon area created by this island is one of diverse marine and bird life, and it can also boast one of the UAE's largest concentrations of mangrove swamps.

Boat trips to Sinaiyyah Island are run from Umm al-Quwain Tourist Centre at the top of the corniche, though you will not be allowed to disembark on the island.

The old fort/museum overlooks the sea on one side and the Creek on the other

FUJAIRAH

As yet, Fujairah has no proven oil resources, but it has two other exploitable advantages – its geography and location. With mountains coming right down to the sea and little or no desert plain, its geography has given it the most beautiful scenic coastline of any of the emirates, an attraction that is gradually drawing more and more tourists. Its location on the east coast of the United Arab Emirates, outside the Arabian Gulf, gives it a more temperate climate than the other emirates, with less extreme temperatures and fewer storms. Ships berthing here are also spared the journey through the Straits of Hormuz, often a politically turbulent waterway.

Before 1976, there was not even a tarmac road connecting Fujairah with the rest of the emirates. The ruling Al-Sharqi family trace their origins back to Yemen and have had many struggles to retain their independence against neighbouring tribes. Fujairah was finally recognised as a separate emirate in 1952, having previously been part of

BULL-FIGHTING

The distinct geography of Fujairah and its lack of deserts have meant that the camel and the falcon play no part in the local traditional lifestyle here. Fujairah is the only emirate that still has no camel race track. Instead, it has developed the sport of bull-fighting, with humped bulls fighting against each other. Fattened up to weigh about 1 tonne, fed on milk, honey and meal, the bulls have a contest of strength, with no blood spilt, to see which can force the other to the ground. This sport is practised at weekends throughout the winter, as indeed it is in neighbouring Oman.

Fujairah, with its dramatic mountains, remains relatively unspoilt

Fujairah's imposing fort overlooks the old town

Sharjah. It joined the United Arab Emirates Federation in 1971. Today, the tarmac road that links Fujairah to the other emirates is a dramatic and scenic dual carriageway through the mountains to reach Masafi. Here, a lively street market lines both sides of the road, selling everything from plants and fruit to carpets. Like most markets, it is at its liveliest after dark when it is cooler and people have free time.

Being such a mountainous emirate, Fujairah is better able to trap its rainfall at dams like Wadi Siji, and then control its use for agriculture in the valleys and fertile coastal plain.

The drive from Dubai takes 2 hours.

Badiyah Mosque

Some 8km (5 miles) north of Khor Fakkan there stands a little white four-domed mosque beside the road. Said to be 400 years old – the oldest still in use in the United Arab Emirates – no wood at all has been used in its construction. It is built entirely of mud.

Fujairah Museum

Now housed in the palace that the present ruler's father vacated in the 1960s, the museum displays a range of ethnographic items including costumes, weapons, tools and household articles.

Tel: (09) 223 1554. Open: Sun–Thur 8am–noon & 4–6pm, Fri 4–6pm. Closed: Sat. Admission charge.

Fujairah old town and fort

Lying behind (north of) the Fujairah Museum, the fort is raised up on a natural outcrop. All around it the ruined mud brick houses of the old town lie part abandoned and part inhabited by subcontinental workers, who often moved into the old houses vacated by nationals in the 1960s when new housing was built.

The camel

Ship of the desert

Life in the desert without a camel is inconceivable; it enters every aspect of daily life. Using a thick comb, Bedouin girls collect winter hair from the camel and this is used for weaving. They spin and dye the wool themselves, and a ram's horn is then used to pull down and tighten the weave. Enormous care is taken of the camels – Ata Allah, the 'Gift of God', is how they are often referred to. Riding camels are invariably female and are often adorned with charms around their necks. A medieval Arabic proverb runs: 'Better than beauty is a camel.'

Camels grazing on acacia tree leaves

Camels live to about 20 years old. They mate for life when they are two, and camel calves are generally born in early autumn. Each owning family brands its yearling camels on the cheek and on the hind quarters, applying yoghurt to the burn to soothe it. Camels are expensive to buy, so the cost involved in slaughtering them at the religious feasts (*eids*) is great. The provision in the Koran is that each family must slaughter according to its means, be it camel, goat or chicken. Camel's milk is an essential part of the diet, and the women make butter and cheese from it, curdled in a camel-leather bag. In the desert, meat was generally only eaten on special occasions like weddings and feast days. The status that used to go with owning a herd of camels is fast evaporating due to changing lifestyles and the fact that they are no longer so profitable.

Supremely adapted to its environment, the camel is designed not to sweat until its body

Female camels are considered faster than males

temperature exceeds 40°C (104°F), thereby conserving its water for long periods, even in excessive heat. The Bedouin relied on the camel's milk long after their own water ran out. The camel can go for months without water as long as it has plants to graze on that have a high water content.

Camel-riding

The extraordinary motion of camel-riding should be experienced at least once, for it is not only backwards and forwards, but also side to side, as if the saddle is about to slip off. The saddle has two wooden pegs to hang on to, one in front, one behind. The camel's getting-up and sitting-down motions take some getting used to. You mount the camel when it is sitting, but the camels are trained to straighten their back legs immediately when they feel your weight, catapulting you forwards without warning, only to be catapulted backwards again once their front legs are straightened. Given that all this happens in a space of seconds, it does not give you much chance to adjust your body weight to the right place.

All Middle Eastern camels are dromedaries (from *dromas*, Greek for 'runner'). The hairier, heavier, two-humped Bactrian variety is only found in colder climes such as eastern Turkey and Central Asia. A group of tourists eyeing some of these camels at the roadside were heard to comment: 'Of course, those aren't riding camels. There's nowhere to sit!'

ABU DHABI AND AL-AIN

Abu Dhabi

Nowhere has the dramatic change of lifestyle for the Emirati people been so marked as in Abu Dhabi. In 1960, there was nothing but a sorry collection of huts where the Manhattan-style skyline of the UAE's capital city now dominates the coast. Representing 80 per cent of the total area of the country, the Emirate of Abu Dhabi has colossal oil wealth, with reserves estimated to last another 100 years, and has the self-assured feel that goes with such a position. It also plays a major part in the UAE's finance and construction industries. Today, a trip to Abu Dhabi need involve no more than a day spent on its stunningly landscaped corniche, strolling around and lunching on a traditional dhow.

Al-Ain, the garden of Abu Dhabi

Al-Ain

Set 160km (100 miles) inland from Abu Dhabi, surrounded by mountains and bordering Oman, Al-Ain is Abu Dhabi's Garden City, yet it is so different that it almost seems like a separate emirate. The population has a high proportion of United Arab Emirates nationals.

Al-Ain has established itself as Abu Dhabi's cultural centre, home to the first United Arab Emirates university and to the Higher Colleges of Technology. Birthplace to Sheikh Zayed, charismatic ruler of Abu Dhabi from 1966 until his death in 2004, it has always been favoured, and blessed with abundant springs and groundwater. Its name means the 'spring' (of water) in Arabic. Archaeologically, Al-Ain is the heartland of Abu Dhabi, and its plentiful water and other attractions were clearly such even in ancient times – earlier civilisations chose it in preference to any other part of the emirates. The wealth of finds is on display in the museum.

Al-Ain Museum

This was the first museum to be established in the emirates back in 1971, opened on the instructions of

FILM FERVOUR

In the courtyard of the Eastern Fort, Sheikh Zayed used to rig up a film projector, connected to the first palace generator, and project against the palace wall. The one film he possessed, an Egyptian film called *The Black Knight*, was shown again and again to the enthralled town inhabitants. 'Sheikh Zayed was always somewhere in our midst,' recalled one of them. 'Not one of us cared that we had only one film, which we knew by heart after several showings.'

Sheikh Zayed, true to his saying 'A country without a past has neither a present nor a future'. Located within the precinct of the Eastern Fort, the museum is very well presented and warrants a long and leisurely visit.
1st St, off Zayed Bin Sultan St. Tel: (03) 764 559. Open: Sat–Thur 9am–7.30pm, Fri 3–7.30pm. Closed: Mon.

Jebel Hafeet

As you approach Jebel Hafeet, especially if this is at night, you will be mesmerised by the near-biblical vision of a series of yellow lights snaking upwards as if to the heavens. This is the illuminated German-constructed road up to Jebel Hafeet, the colossal 1,240m (4,068ft) rock outcrop that dominates the south of Al-Ain, a must-see for any visitor. Sunset is the best time, and even eagles and vultures can sometimes be spotted gliding in the updraughts.
The drive from Dubai takes some 90 minutes.

There are magnificent views from the top of Jebel Hafeet

Getting away from it all

Dubai offers a surprising range and variety of opportunities to get away from the city. You do not even have to go very far to escape into the desert, the mountains or remote wadis, where you are likely to be the only person there.

Ad-Dour

This remarkably extensive archaeological site belongs within the territory of Umm Al-Quwain and is about a one- to two-hour drive from central Dubai, depending on traffic. It offers the unique interest of being the only Hellenistic (Greek-influenced) site in the United Arab Emirates. It is also an attractive spot for walking, away from the crowds and with shady trees to picnic under. On Fridays, it can get a little busy as local Arab families like to use the excavators' tracks as a racecourse for their children's sand buggies.

The site covers an area about 1km (1/2 mile) wide and 4km (2 1/2 miles) long. Scattered about are literally hundreds of tombs, a fort dated to the 4th century AD and a simple temple, still standing over 2m (7ft) high, dated to between 100 BC and AD 100, which

The temple remains at Ad-Dour

Easy walking terrain at Jebel Buheis

was discovered by archaeologists in 1989. It has friezes of meandering vine leaves still with traces of yellows and ochres. The settlement is thought to have declined and disappeared when the creek on which it originally sat silted up with tidal movements, thereby cutting it off from its lifeline, the sea. The sand is still littered with shells. *The landmark to help pinpoint the site is the Emirates Petrol Station on the right-hand side of the main highway as you head towards Ras Al-Khaimah, roughly 10km (6¼ miles) from the Umm Al-Quwain roundabout turn-off. Just 200m (220yds) before the petrol station, look out for a small track that leads up onto a mound overlooking the road, with some insignificant-looking stone foundations on top, now thought to be a Governor's House because of its exceptional size and design. From here, the track continues inland, through a makeshift gate in the fence, which you should close behind you. After about 1km (½ mile), you can stop among the red dunes beside two tall ghaf trees. The track presents no problems for a carefully driven car.*

Jebel Buheis

Located within one of Sharjah's inland enclaves, this pleasant spot is just over an hour's drive from Dubai City. It therefore offers an easy escape to the countryside, where the terrain makes walking possible in the gently rolling hills. For added interest, this is the site of an ancient necropolis recently excavated by a German team, and you can also keep an eye out for the marine fossils scattered about.

The skeletons of 180 humans dating to the third millennium BC were unearthed here in some 19 tombs, the women buried with large quantities of necklaces, pearls and precious stones, suggesting they were very rich.

Picnicking is easy here, and you will almost always have the place to yourself. *The site lies some 10km (6¼ miles) north of the Madam roundabout. From the Jebel Faya turn-off, the main road continues south for another 11.5km (7 miles) to reach Jebel Buheis, where the track leads off towards the rocky outcrop near the tall radio mast. Take the track that leads in between two farms to the mountain, heading for the guardian's conical tent. This track is exactly 1.5km (1 mile) after the ADNOC petrol station (on the right) if you are coming from the Madam roundabout.*

The inhospitable but beautiful Empty Quarter

Liwa

The Liwa oasis is the ultimate remote destination if you want to experience a taste of the sands of the Empty Quarter, one of the world's largest deserts. A five-hour drive from Dubai, the journey should not be undertaken lightly. It requires four-wheel drive, a stay of two nights and plenty of planning, as it lies within Abu Dhabi territory, 200km (124 miles) south of Abu Dhabi city. Before 1960, the journey had to be done on foot and camel, so it took five days of gruelling hardship. The oasis is in fact formed from an arc of 40 to 60 villages. A simple rest house offers an alternative to camping.

Ras Al-Khaimah

Geographically and scenically favoured, with a convergence of sand, sea, mountains and plains, Ras Al-Khaimah (Head of the Tent) is the greenest and boasts the most fertile agricultural soil of all the emirates. The pace of life here is pleasantly unhurried, with little of the frenetic commercialism of Dubai and Abu Dhabi. There is the highest number of indigenous Arabs of any of the emirates. Ras Al-Khaimah has always perceived itself as somewhat apart from the others, and initially stayed out of the United Arab Emirates Federation until it realised the extent of federal aid it would receive as a result of joining.

The drive from Dubai takes about 2 hours, and to do it justice you will need to spend the night in one of the luxury hotels or else camp in the foothills of the mountains.

Husn Shimmel (Sheba's Palace)

Here, you will enter the largest concentration of archaeological sites to be found anywhere in the emirates. To reach Sheba's Palace, you must head for the slight cleft on the rock where a sort of path becomes apparent. The ascent takes about ten minutes but is not difficult, although the terrain is a little loose and requires proper footwear.

The fine medieval Islamic hill fort and defensive settlement is on a natural plateau overlooking the plain towards the sea. The name Sheba probably comes from a misinterpretation of the Arabic 'Qasr Al-Zaba', which means 'Palace of the High Plateau'. The site has never been properly excavated, but the pottery found here dates it to the 16th and 17th centuries. Once at the top, the most impressive aspect of the site is its complex water system, with oblong cisterns to preserve vital rainwater and a large well. The charm of the site, however, lies less in its ruins than in its dramatic position on a naturally defensive plateau, with the spectacular mountain backdrop and the surprisingly green vegetation. The best time to visit is in spring after the first heavy rains, when the hilltop will be covered in grass and tiny flowers.

Some 6km (4 miles) north of Ras Al-Khaimah town, on the way towards Rams, take the track to the right, 4km (2½ miles) after the Emirates petrol station. Follow this for just over 3km (2 miles), past some tombs and a pyramid-shaped rock, to reach the green water tower where you should park.

Shimmel Necropolis

Retracing your path back towards a distinctive pyramid-shaped rock, you will come to this area of tombs. Extending for some 3km (2 miles) along the base of the mountains and

The hill of Sheba's Palace in Ras Al-Khaimah

around another weird pyramid-shaped rock of a lighter colour is the most extensive and important concentration of ancient tombs in the emirates. In the 1970s and 1980s, over 60 tombs from the second millennium BC were identified here by British and German excavators. Drive to the shade of the trees behind the pyramid-shaped rock for a leisurely picnic or to camp in the evening. The spot is very peaceful, away from any villages, and you can spend many hours exploring the area and especially the pyramid rock itself, which conceals some extraordinary tunnels and caves. The ground is littered with pottery shards and huge numbers of shells, revealing that the sea once covered this area and also that shellfish comprised a major part of the local diet, notably the mangrove mud snail, a favourite food in ancient times.

ANCIENT DIET

Studies of the bones found in the Shimmel Necropolis tombs showed that the locals suffered severe teeth and jaw problems as a result of the high consumption of sugary dates. Life expectancy was only around 30–35 and the bones show that 45 per cent of children died very young. The other contents of the tombs, like jewellery, weapons and pottery, are on show in Ras Al-Khaimah's Fort Museum.

Tel: (07) 233 3411. Open: Wed–Mon 8am–noon & 4–7pm (summer); 10am–5pm (winter). Closed: Tues. Admission charge.

One of the distinctive pyramid-shaped rocky hills at Shimmel

Wadi Hulw, the 'Beautiful Valley'

Wadi Hulw

This trip requires four-wheel drive and an overnight camping stay, but you will be rewarded by some of the most beautiful and remote mountain scenery anywhere in the emirates. The name Wadi Hulw means 'Beautiful Valley', and it is located near Hatta in Fujairah.

Here, you will see unspoilt views, lots of water flowing in the wadi bed, and lush vegetation with flowering pink oleander. Look out for the extensive ruined settlement on your left, with thick defensive walls and tombs into which you can climb down. A few kilometres further on into the valley, you will see another extensive settlement to your right, set in a grassy dell between two hills. This is thought to be an ancient copper-mining village, and occasional pieces of jet-black slag, as well as the tell-tale green-tinged stones, can be found. According to recent studies, very little copper remains in these mountains today. *From the Hatta Fort roundabout, head north 10km (6 miles) past Huwaylat, then straight on to Muna'i some 4km (2½ miles) further on. On the outskirts of Muna'i, look out for a generating station to the right of the road beside a large pylon. Take the road here past a repair garage raised up on your left, and head towards the mountains eastwards, aiming for the electricity pylons in the distance, crossing the wadi bed to reach them at what is clearly the entrance to Wadi Hulw. After 5.6km (3½ miles), past the settlement of Hulw and its extensive quarry works, the scenery improves dramatically.*

When to go

For five months of the year, from November until early March, the climate in Dubai is wonderful. Between May and September it is terribly hot, while in the months between these two seasons – October, March and April – the temperatures are somewhat more bearable.

High season

From November through to the end of February, the days are generally bright and balmy with perfect temperatures around the mid-20s°C (75°F). The evenings are a little fresh (averaging around 15°C/59°F), requiring an extra layer like a jacket or a sweater, but never a coat. Naturally, this is the period that qualifies as high season in the hotels, when flights are more expensive and room rates are at their priciest. Christmas and New Year are the absolute peak times when the holiday season coincides with what is guaranteed to be perfect weather, and flights can be very expensive unless booked several months in advance. The sea temperature hovers between 21°C (70°F) and 24°C (75°F), making it a little chillier than the 26°C (79°F) to which the hotel pools are generally heated. However, if you have come from the UK and are used to sea temperatures of well below 20°C (68°F), then it will still seem pleasantly warm.

A traditional Ramadan tent offers some protection from the sun

Mid-season

In the months between summer and winter (October, March and April), the climate is definitely on the hot side, with temperatures into the low to mid-30s°C (88–97°F) during the day, dropping to the mid- to high 20s°C (75–85°F) at night. The first part of October can still be surprisingly hot, and swimming in the sea is like

During the mid-season, the sea is a perfect temperature for swimming

entering a perfect bath temperature. Locals say the magic date when the weather gets cooler is 20 October. Likewise, in March, the first part of the month is still fairly cool, then quite suddenly, from around 15 March onwards, the temperature shoots up dramatically. Prices in these mid-season months are noticeably lower than in the high season, so it can be a good time to visit, as long as you stay out of the sun over the 11am–3pm period.

Low season

Unsurprisingly, the cheapest months in which to visit Dubai are the hot summer months of May to September, with July and August the hottest of all. Daytime highs are often in the low to mid-40s°C (low 100s°F), and humidity can reach 100 per cent. Even in the evenings it does not drop below the mid- to high 30s°C (93–102°F). As for the sea temperature, it gets to around 37°C (99°F), but reaching the water's edge across the baking sand is a major challenge, and not to be attempted barefoot. A visit at these times will have to be spent in the air-conditioned malls and in the shaded areas of the temperature-controlled hotel pool.

For visits during Ramadan, *see p135*.

Rainfall

Rain can strike Dubai at any time, even in August, although it is rare. The winter months are more likely to get rain, and when there is a heavy downpour, chaos ensues, with myriad traffic accidents and power cuts. The roads flood quickly because there is no drainage, and in the mountainous Hatta area, flash floods in the wadis can be treacherous.

In the autumn and spring months, the mornings can be very foggy and humid, but by mid-morning the fog has usually cleared.

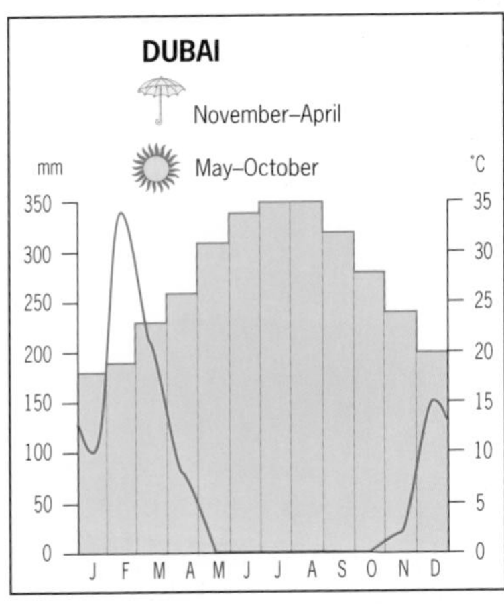

WEATHER CONVERSION CHART

25.4mm = 1 inch

°F = 1.8 × °C + 32

Getting around

Dubai is a very car-orientated place, with an extraordinarily well-developed road network, and good and clear signposting. There are no trains, and local buses are crowded and uncomfortable. Many of the bigger hotels run courtesy buses for guests. The Dubai Metro, the largest driverless metro system in the world, opened in September 2009, with two of its projected four lines now complete.

By taxi

For a visitor staying just a few days in Dubai, the taxi is the simplest way of travelling. Taxis are relatively cheap and ubiquitous, with over 5,000 of them operating in the city. The standard pick-up fare is Dh3–Dh3.50, except if you are within the airport area, where the automatic fare is Dh20 minimum to anywhere. There are now women-only taxis, recognisable by their pink roofs and interiors. They are all much the same and are run by the Dubai Transport Corporation. All taxis are

Taxis are cheap and plentiful and can be found outside all shopping malls

The camel highway code must be obeyed

metered and fitted with global positioning systems (GPS). You can summon one by calling the **Dubai Transport Corporation** (*Tel: 208 0808*).

By car

Compared with other parts of the Middle East, the standard of driving in Dubai is relatively good and the traffic police are in evidence issuing fines. The main problem is speed because the excellent road network seems to encourage drivers to travel at high speed, with the eight-lane Sheikh Zayed Highway particularly prone to lane weaving and high-speed crashes. The United Arab Emirates has one of the highest road accident death rates per capita in the world. As a visitor, the sensible precaution is to stick to the Beach Road for getting to the centre of Dubai, and to avoid the peak times of 7–9am and 5–7pm.

Car hire

If you are staying for more than a long weekend, plan to do a few day trips or even drive into Oman, then car hire is well worth it and very cheap. The rate includes unlimited mileage for a week including collision damage waiver for the smallest class of car. There are many firms offering car hire. **Thrifty** (with 15 offices in Dubai; *www.thriftyuae.com*) is one of the best and cheapest, with branches all over the place, including in most of the malls. There is no extra charge for collection and pick-up at different locations within the city.
You can drive a hire car into Oman, but you must inform the car hire company at the time of booking, and there is an additional charge for insurance. The only documentation you need is your passport and your national driver's licence.

Accommodation

For Dubai accommodation, luxury hotels are the first thing that most people think of, and it is true that the city has more five-star hotels per hectare than anywhere else in the world. There are other cheaper options, however, such as hotel apartments that are good for longer stays, and there is even a youth hostel. There are no official campsites, but camping rough is allowed on the beaches away from the city, or anywhere inland in the mountains, wadis and desert.

Hotels

Faced with a bewildering array of choice from the top-of-the-range 'seven-star' Burj Al-Arab Hotel, right down to the one-star places in Deira, the initial reaction by the visitor can be confusion and a sense of being spoilt for choice. The first thing to decide is how much you want to pay, and second where you want to be.

A luxury five-star beach hotel near Dubai Marina

City hotels

If you want proximity to the souks and the cultural heritage, the best places are the city hotels of Bur Dubai, Deira and Bastakia. Most are situated along the Creek on the Deira side, but now there is a handful of traditional hotels in the Bastakia quarter on the Bur Dubai side. These are in restored old wind tower courtyard houses, a new development in Dubai, offering something closer to an authentic Arabian experience. They do not have pools or sports facilities, but make an interesting contrast to beach hotels. It can be quite fun to have a couple of nights in a traditional place before transferring to one of the beach hotels.

Beach hotels

If you are on a long weekend break for rest and relaxation, you should look no further than one of the hotels along Jumeirah Beach, which are almost entirely four- and five-star. They all offer excellent facilities with beautifully

The wave design of the Jumeirah Beach Hotel

landscaped grounds, temperature-controlled pools and immaculate sandy beaches with showers. The sports facilities are superb, with tennis courts, watersports, gyms, saunas and health clubs with massage and beauty centres. Most have galleries of shops with local clothing and souvenirs, several restaurants from formal dining to poolside snack places, car hire outlets and tour operators, where you can book a range of trips from city tours to desert experiences. Courtesy buses are often laid on to popular destinations like the Creek, the centre of Dubai or the airport.

Business hotels

If your trip is for business, establish where your business will mostly be conducted and book a hotel as close as possible so that you do not waste time in traffic jams getting to meetings. Most of the business hotels are in Deira, such as the Hyatt Regency Hotel on the Deira shoreline, or the Sheraton or InterContinental, both of which are situated on the Deira Creek.

Novelty hotels

Burj Al-Arab Hotel is the ultimate novelty hotel, often called a 'seven-star' hotel and in a league of its own for luxury (*see p79 & p167*). Late 2008 saw the opening of Atlantis, on the Palm Jumeirah, complete with some underwater bedroom suites, its own Dolphin Bay and 17 hectares (42 acres) of tropical theme park with ziggurat water slides. Desert hotels are all the

Luxury lounges are typical of hotel lobbies such as this one at the Jumeirah Beach Hotel

rage, and the ultimate is the Al-Maha Desert Resort and Spa, 45km (28 miles) outside the city (*see p172*). Oryx graze within sight of the hotel, as this is the Dubai Desert Conservation Reserve, Dubai's premier eco-resort, offering wildlife drives and sunset camel rides. The other main desert hotel is Bab Al-Shams Desert Resort and Spa, in the desert inland from Jebel Ali, with a desert medina, Dead Sea toiletries and even falconry displays (*see p171*).

Hotel apartments

This is the favoured option for people working in Dubai on short-term contracts or for expatriates first arriving in the city who use an apartment as a base from which to explore and find a villa or flat to rent. Most of the hotel apartments are in the central areas, either in Deira or on the Bur Dubai side of the Creek. Some are quite luxurious and linked to the top hotels like the Marriott, the Hyatt Regency or the Savoy, while others are at a more standard level like the Golden Sands. All come fully furnished and have a cleaning service, and the advantages are that they are cheaper than a hotel and you will feel more at home and have more space than in a hotel room.

Hostel

The **Dubai Youth Hostel** offers the cheapest accommodation in town (*see p160*). It is the only one in Dubai, but there are others in Sharjah (*Tel: (06) 522 5070*), Fujairah (*Tel: (09) 222 2347*) and Khor Fakkan (*Tel: (09) 237 0886*). There are about 100 beds, mainly in simple but clean four-bed dormitories,

and the cost is around Dh50–Dh70 per night including breakfast. Bookings from single women will be turned down in favour of men.
Located about a 15-minute drive from Dubai International Airport, on the Deira side of the Creek near the Al Mulla Plaza. Tel: 298 8151.

Camping

The time of year is the main constraint on camping, and you should only consider camping in the winter months between November and the end of February. Even in the spring and autumn months, it tends to be unbearably hot. On the beaches, a permit is required and these are issued free of charge by the Dubai Municipality. In practice, you will not be asked to show it unless you are drunk and disorderly. With car hire so cheap, camping is certainly one way of keeping your costs right down.

PRICES

Accommodation prices are highly seasonal, with top prices paid in the winter months from November to the end of February, especially at Christmas and New Year. At *eid* (religious festival) periods, prices are also very high. The worldwide financial crisis has meant fewer overseas visitors, and prices have had to drop to lure them back. In the hot summer months, prices drop by up to 40 per cent from the published room rate. For Internet reservations, consult *www.dubaitourism.ae* or *www.booking.com*

A shisha tent in the lobby of the Jumeirah Hilton

Food and drink

Dubai offers literally everything in the food and drink line, as you would expect from such a cosmopolitan place, where most nationalities rub shoulders. Restaurants cover cuisine from five continents, and range from the upmarket dining rooms of the top hotels to the simple street shawarma *(spit-roasted lamb in pitta bread) stands. Eating has always held an important place in the Arab world, and is viewed as a social affair, with large families gathering and eating together from communal dishes.*

Arabic food

There are many restaurants throughout Dubai that serve what is known as Arabic food but is in practice Lebanese. The range of meze starters includes stuffed vine leaves, aubergine and chickpea dips, and hot stuffed spinach or cheese pastries, all of which are excellent for vegetarians. These are followed by kebab-style main courses, and sweet, sticky puddings made with nuts and honey. The meze are eaten with flat Arabic bread, and the main course and puddings would traditionally have been eaten with the fingers.

Emirati cuisine is much more difficult to find, although some of the hotel restaurants are now offering the occasional local dish on their menus. Typical local fare is roasted lamb stuffed with rice, which is spiced with cinnamon, turmeric, almonds and pistachios. Dried limes are commonly used here, too, as a flavouring in soups and stews, a reflection of the Persian influence. Pork is not eaten by Muslims because the Koran states that it is an unclean meat. In Dubai, however, you will find pork on the menu, and even in supermarkets you can find pork in separate areas from the rest of the meat.

A plate of tempting fresh fruit

Beachside cafés are perfect places to relax

Alcohol

Dubai has a liberal attitude towards alcohol, and hotels and clubs are issued with a liquor licence that enables them to serve alcohol in their restaurants and bars. Alcohol is not, however, freely available in shops, and there are no off-licences. You cannot buy alcohol over the counter unless you are a resident who has been issued with a liquor licence. In practice, many Muslims in Dubai do drink, and visit the bars just as much as Westerners.

FASTING

Unlike the rest of the Arabian Peninsula, Dubai is surprisingly unaffected by the 30-day Ramadan fast, and food and alcohol are freely available in the hotels and restaurants during daylight hours. The only restriction you will notice is that eating and drinking in public during daylight hours are forbidden, so there can be no walking around drinking from a water bottle, for example. In the evenings, however, Ramadan is wonderful and adds an extra dimension to any visit, with the *iftar* (fast-breaking) celebrations and a livelier nightlife than usual.

Entertainment

Eating out in fine restaurants and drinking in bars form a large part of the entertainment in Dubai. Bars and nightclubs are easy to find and there is a good selection of cinemas and concerts, plus one or two theatres. Visitors interested in fashion will be spoilt for choice at the shopping malls.

Eating out

There are so many special venues in Dubai, each with a different ambience, that you would be hard-pressed to try them all. Probably one of the most memorable is a dinner cruise on the Creek, offered by several companies (*see pp163–5*).

Shishas for sale in Deira

Bars and nightclubs

The nightlife in Dubai tends to start late, with 9pm being the earliest that anyone sets out. Most places only really get going after 11pm. Wednesdays, Thursdays and Fridays are the busiest nights, because of the weekend falling on either Thursday/Friday or Friday/Saturday. Closing time is anything between 1 and 3am. The dress code tends to be quite smart, so you will need something more formal than jeans and a T-shirt. Many nightclubs will have a belly dancer, singer and live band.

Cinemas

All the shopping malls have cinema complexes, many with ten or more screens. Even so, the screenings of the popular films get very crowded. The Ibn Battuta Mall (*see p52*) has an IMAX screen, the first in the area. Listings can be found in the local papers (*see p153*). Censorship of explicit sexual scenes is thorough, and all films have Arabic

DVD film releases on sale

subtitles. The air conditioning can be icy, so go prepared. The Cinestar Gold Cinemas in the Mall of the Emirates are the height of luxury, with reclining seats in pairs, private tables and superior snacks (*see p164*).

Concerts and theatre

Performers on tour come regularly to Dubai, so there is a professional performance to be seen at least once a month. There are classical concerts as well as pop concerts, with the latter including popular performers such as Lionel Ritchie and Rod Stewart. Comedy nights are held about once every two months, with international stand-up comedians. The big five-star hotels are the usual venues.

Theatre is a little more limited, with plays coming on tour every now and again. However, the indigenous talent is growing now with two local theatres, the first at the Madinat Theatre within Madinat Jumeirah (*see p169*), and the second at the new Dubai Community Theatre and Arts Centre within the Mall of the Emirates (*see p164*).

Fashion shows

Dubai prides itself on its frequent fashion shows – commonly held in the shopping malls and hotels, especially during the Dubai Shopping Festival – which all help to cement the city's image as the best place to shop for clothes in the Middle East. Sometimes there may be as many as 30 shows a month.

SHISHA

Also popularly known as hubble-bubble or hookah pipes, the correct Arabic name for the shisha water-pipe is *narguileh*. Arabs enjoy them before, during and after meals, and often flavour the tobacco with fruits like apple, strawberry or grape. During Ramadan, the pipes are especially popular. Once requested, the water-pipe is brought to you and lit by the waiter. You have to keep puffing quite regularly to make sure it stays alight, but the sensation is very pleasurable, with the water making the smoke much smoother. Most adult visitors give it a try.

Shopping

Shopping is the national pastime in Dubai, indulged in by all nationalities. The mall culture has cast its spell on most residents and many would freely admit that there is nothing they love more than to stroll in a leisurely fashion around the malls eyeing up potential purchases. Whole families go out, especially at night, to window-shop, sip coffee in the cafés or just to enjoy the pleasant air-conditioned, dust- and sand-free atmosphere. Most shops are open 10am–10pm.

IN DUBAI

Best buys

Gold is the first thing that springs to mind for a best buy, and a visit to the Gold Souk (*see pp62–3*) is virtually a must for all visitors. The range of choice and the relatively affordable prices make it hard to resist a purchase. Carpets are probably the next best buy, especially if you venture to the souks in

Glitzy souvenirs for sale

Dubai's shopping malls often have lavish interiors

Sharjah. The close proximity to Iran means that there is always a ready supply of Persian carpets.

Other items unique to Dubai that will serve as distinctive souvenirs are antiques from the pre-oil era, best found either in the souks or in some of the specialist galleries (*see pp68–9*). These may include old silver jewellery or old wooden chests and carved doors.

DUBAI DUTY FREE

If you never quite got around to gift shopping on your trip, you may be saved by the Dubai Airport duty-free shopping area. Here, the shops offer a range of items from clothing and watercolours to coffee pots.

Pashminas make good souvenirs as do shisha water-pipes, although they are rather cumbersome in your luggage.

One of the simplest, easiest and cheapest souvenirs or gifts to take home is fresh spices and herbs from the souk, excellent value and useful, too.

Malls

The malls offer convenience and a sanitised environment in which to shop. They have covered parking and sell everything. There is usually a hypermarket, such as Carrefour, as the anchor shop, then a number of clothing shops ranging from Gap, Next, etc. to the top fashion boutiques like Prada and Givenchy. The Dubai Mall and Mall of the Emirates are considered the two most exclusive malls for designer clothing. Big retailers like Debenhams and Marks & Spencer are generally present in the malls. Prices are rarely lower than in the UK.

BEYOND DUBAI

Many residents who are familiar with Dubai's shopping delights still choose to frequent the Sharjah malls instead, where prices are often a little lower. For unusual but authentic gifts, Sharjah's traditional Souk Al-Arsah (*see p107*) is hard to beat, and never suffers from the overcrowding that sometimes afflicts Dubai. Sharjah is also unbeatable for its furniture warehouses, especially those selling attractive Indian pieces such as dowry chests. The three main ones are Pinky's, Lucky's and Khan's, all of which are in Sharjah's industrial area.

Street markets

Another shopping experience beyond Dubai is the street markets spread out on either side of the road. There are two major ones: the first as you approach Hatta, shortly before entering Hatta town, and the second at Dhaid, on the road to Fujairah. Both of these are excellent for traditional clay ornaments, carpets, plants, fruit and vegetables.

Bargaining

Bargaining is still the norm in all souks and shopping areas outside the malls of Dubai and the UAE in general. It is expected, and if you do not indulge you will simply be overcharged and spoil prices for the next foreigner who comes along. Your opening bid should be around 50 per cent of the seller's initial price. He will, of course, reject this, and you then both work towards something around two-thirds of the first asking price. The more you buy, the better the discount will be, and if you begin to frequent a particular shop, the owner will generally reward your loyalty with lower prices. It is important to remain polite and calm throughout, with no displays of temper or frustration, otherwise the price will certainly go up.

Shipping

If you buy something heavy and/or bulky such as a chest or a carpet, which you obviously cannot transport back yourself, most shops are able to arrange shipping for you. Air freight is faster but more expensive, while sea freight is cheaper but can take many weeks. For large items of furniture, sea freight is probably the only option, but air freight is better for smaller items that are needed more quickly.

Computers and electrical goods

Prices for high-tech electrical goods such as TVs are often cheaper here than elsewhere, but you must take extra care to make sure they will work in your home country, and also check that the warranty will be internationally valid.

Secondhand goods

A market in secondhand, vintage or pre-loved goods is pretty much the only sector where Dubai is lacking. So if people have goods they want to sell, for example when they're leaving the country after a working stint here, they place adverts on the noticeboards of the supermarkets such as Spinneys and Choithrams, or alternatively post online classified adverts. One of the best of these sites is *www.expatwoman.com*

Supermarkets

The Indian chain Choithrams is the biggest with over 12 branches, followed by Spinneys, which probably has the best quality food and has the widest range of choices for vegetarians. The French Carrefour hypermarket also has several branches across the city.

Snacks and souvenirs for sale in a typical market

Sport and leisure

There can be few places as well provided with sport and leisure facilities as Dubai. You name it, it's available. As a visitor, you will have ample opportunity at your hotel to sample a good range of facilities – all the four- and five-star places have tennis courts, watersports, health clubs and fitness classes in addition to their private beaches and swimming pools.

Adventure sports

Dune-driving, wadi-bashing, rock climbing and skydiving are the ones that spring to mind. If you are a visitor, these are best arranged through your hotel; your resident tour operator will have all the contacts to set it up for you. The Hatta Fort Hotel (*see p172*) makes an excellent base. If you are a resident, your best bet is to find like-minded experienced adventurers and go with them the first few times.

Dubai's sports shops are well stocked

The golf courses are immaculately kept

Birdwatching

The magnificently green and well-watered parks and golf courses have lured many bird species to Dubai, and over 400 species pass through here en route when migrating from Africa to Central Asia. The Wildlife Sanctuary at Ras Al-Khor is excellent for flamingos, and on a winter's day you can spot up to 1,500 of them. Small parties can visit free of charge and watch from the three hides (*see p49*).

Cycling

Dubai is not an easy place in which to cycle, and this is the reason why you will see almost no cyclists on the roads. There is safe cycling along the pedestrian Creekside paths, but most of the parks do not permit you to bring your own bike, although some, like Safa Park (*see p71*), rent out tandems or family bikes seating four that are quite fun but surprisingly hard work.

Golf

This is probably the sport from which Dubai has most made its name, a feat it achieved by initiating the Dubai Desert Classic at the beautiful Emirates Golf Club, one of the world's richest tournaments. The tournament runs for four days and is held in late February/early March.

Dubai is now seen as one of the world's premier golfing destinations, with superb facilities and perfect weather in the winter months. Floodlighting also ensures that some of the courses can be played after dark in the hotter months (*see pp84–5*). The emirate has many top-class golf

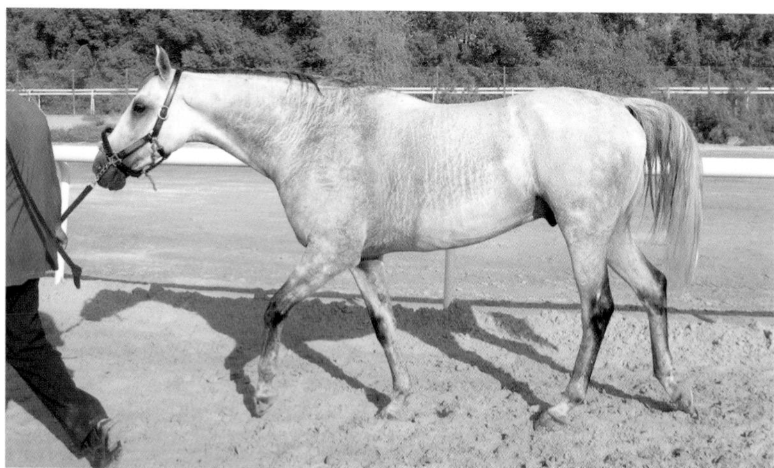

The Arabian horse is a fine racer

courses, some of which, like the Desert Course (*see p170*) designed by Ian Baker-Finch and the Montgomerie (*see p171*) designed by Colin Montgomerie, have luxurious rooms in their affiliated hotels to lure wealthy golfers to this golfing paradise.

Hiking and running

Walking within the city is difficult anywhere except in the parks or along the Creekside promenade. Consequently, for anything like serious walking, you will need to head out towards the mountains. Just an hour's drive from Dubai you can go for excellent walks, ranging from short, easy strolls along flat wadi beds, to all-day treks to spectacular viewpoints. There is an excellent locally-produced booklet called *Oman Trekking Explorer* which gives detailed routes and maps, and the United Arab Emirates *Offroad Explorer* booklet also gives information on hiking routes. November to the end of February are the best months for proper mountain hiking, but always go well prepared, taking plenty of water and provisions, because there is no mountain rescue service if you get into difficulties. If you are a newcomer, go in the company of an experienced walker who knows the terrain.

The Hash House Harriers, the worldwide group of social running clubs, often better known for their socialising than their running, are well represented here. There are four different groups, including the Creek Hash House Harriers (*www.creekhash.net*), and the Desert Hash House Harriers who meet on Sundays (*www.deserthash.org*). Runs last about 45–60 minutes and are around courses that have been laid out by a 'hare' in advance.

Horse riding and polo

Dubai has several riding stables where you can take lessons. The state-of-the-art **Dubai Polo and Equestrian Club** (*www.poloclubdubai.com*) has 300 livery stables, lessons for all levels, a tack shop, and a clubhouse with restaurants and bars. Polo is also taught here and there are two full-size pitches. International polo matches are played at the **Ghantoot Polo and Racing Club** (*Sheikh Maktoum Rd, Jazira. Tel: (02) 562 9050*). Here there are six pitches and full club facilities with pool, gym, sauna and restaurant so that the family can relax while you play.

Skiing and winter sports

The arrival of the region's first ski slope, set within the Mall of the Emirates, has transformed the lives of many residents (*see p85*). Some expatriates now ski regularly in their lunch break, while local families have the chance to experience snow and temperatures of –5°C (23°F) for the first time in their lives. In addition to skiing, you can toboggan down the bobsleigh run, or just roll around and throw snowballs. Rates are pricey but include hire of equipment.

Watersports are on offer at the big beach hotels

Spectator sports

The two spectator sports that are hugely popular in Dubai are camel racing (*see pp98–9*) and horse racing, both based outside the city. Early morning around 7.30am is the best time to catch the action, and even if there are no actual races, you will always see the animals out exercising on the tracks – a photo opportunity not to be missed.

Watersports

Scuba diving, snorkelling, sailing, surfing, waterskiing, kite-surfing, jet-skiing and speedboating are all activities that can be arranged through your hotel. The local booklet *Underwater Explorer* has details of the best places for diving and snorkelling, and there are over 12 diving centres and clubs to choose from.

Well-being

Dubai takes its health and beauty seriously, and there is a great variety of beauty salons, health spas and clubs offering the full range of beauty treatments as well as massage, pilates, reiki, t'ai chi and yoga. Cleopatra's Spa, tucked away behind the Wafi Mall, is one of the more exotic, designed like something out of ancient Egypt, complete with silk cushions to loll on in the relaxation area (*see p166*).

Sea life and wildlife

The dugong are often accidentally caught in fishing nets

Sea life

Beachcombing can provide hours of amusement, with many shells washed up on the shoreline. You can preserve the colours of your shell collection by giving it a thorough wash, allowing it to dry, then giving it a light coating of baby oil.

The mammals found in the sea here are dugong, also known as sea cows. They are large, heavy creatures weighing up to 500kg (1,100lb) and were traditionally mistaken for mermaids or sirens by local sailors. Shallow water grazers, they feed on sea-grass. Accidental net capture is the biggest threat to the dugong, and its meat is still highly prized by some in the Gulf. Dolphins are also found and, unlike the dugong, they are not under threat of extinction; they feed on fish, octopus and squid, which are still plentiful.

Sea dangers

The dangers of the sea can be exaggerated and you should certainly not become paranoid about all the potentially poisonous and fatal creatures that lurk there – your chances of encountering them are very small. Plenty of sharks exist, but they do not come in close to shore; stingrays can in theory be stepped on when they are buried in the sand, but local doctors say it almost never happens; lionfish and stonefish can be seen when diving or snorkelling along coral reefs and rocky shores, but you would have to step on their sharp spines quite heavily to hurt yourself; sea snakes have a fatal bite, but their jaws are so small that they cannot get their teeth into anything bigger than a child's finger; and jellyfish can sting, but most pharmacies sell jellyfish-sting sprays.

THE ARABIAN LEOPARD

The Arabian Leopard Trust was set up in the early 1990s to protect these few remaining rare creatures, hunted to near extinction by local farmers. The male weighs 30kg (66lb) and the female 20kg (44lb), making them smaller than other African and Asian leopards. They are mainly solitary, though pairs come together for mating sessions that last for around five days. Gestation takes 100 days, after which anything from one to four cubs are born. The Arabian leopards' natural prey of *tahr* (mountain goat) and mountain gazelle are also near extinction. As a result, they turn to domestic stock, such as goats, which explains their unpopularity. Their lifespan is 8 years in the wild, 12 in captivity. A breeding programme is in place in Sharjah.

Wildlife

Reptiles like the Dhubb lizard and the desert monitor have always been native to the Arabian Peninsula. Most of the mammals, like the oryx, desert cat, fox and ostrich, came across from Africa eons ago when Arabia and Africa were connected. As a visitor, it is the insect life that you are most likely to meet, especially if you camp out in the desert. Scorpions do exist and you should always keep the tent zipped up and check your shoes in the morning. The large black ones are the least poisonous – it is the small sandy ones you should avoid.

The alert gaze of the desert monitor

Children

It is difficult to imagine anywhere more like a children's paradise than Dubai. Children are welcome everywhere, at all hotels and restaurants, and you will never experience eating tantrums as just about every place offers children's menus. As well as the pleasures of the beach and the pool, most hotels have playgrounds, children's activities and babysitting. Even the health clubs attached to the hotels usually have kids' clubs. The locally published booklet Family Explorer *gives full details of venues and activities.*

Skiing, tobogganing and ice rinks

The full range of winter sports is on offer in this semi-tropical climate. The ski slope at the Mall of the Emirates is great for introducing children to the delights of snow and skiing (*see p85*).

The desert comes in handy as a sandpit

The beginners' slopes are nice and gentle, and they can have lessons to get a feel for it or maybe to practise for the real thing on a skiing holiday elsewhere. Ski and kit hire is included in the price. There are two ice rinks, one at Al-Nasr Leisureland and the other at the Hyatt Regency Hotel (*see p86 & p161*).

Theme parks

Dubai offers an extraordinary range of entertainment for children, with Magic Planet, within the Mall of the Emirates (*see p53*), an excellent choice. Many of the shopping malls have special areas dedicated to children, such as the Encounter Zone in the Wafi Mall (*see p53*), where they are divided into pre-teens and the younger ones. Children can often be left in these areas under supervision while the adults go and do some serious shopping.

Water parks

The Wild Wadi Waterpark (*see pp86–7*) has an ingeniously designed series of

HEALTH AND SAFETY

Dubai is one of the safest destinations in the world for children. There have never been any reported incidents of assault or molestation. Dubai is a clean place and the swimming pools are immaculately maintained. The biggest health risk is the sun, and it is vitally important not to let children stay out in it between 11am and 3pm. Make sure they are always protected with waterproof suncream of at least 25 SPF (sun protection factor) as 80 per cent of skin damage is caused before the age of 18.

rides, from the gentle to the terrifying, to cater for all ages. It is easy to spend an entire day here, grazing on the snacks and fast food. Al-Nasr Leisureland also has a water park (*see p86*), although it is not as frenetic as the Wild Wadi.

Zoo

Dubai Zoo may be enjoyable for young children as you can get much closer to the animals than in most zoos because it is so old and overcrowded (*see pp74–5*). Older children may find the conditions a little disturbing, depending on their level of sensitivity.

Children love the special water toys

Essentials

Arriving

By air

Dubai's own airline, **Emirates** (*Tel: 214 4444. www.emirates.com*), runs services to over 70 destinations and is rated as one of the best in the world. **Etihad Airways** (*www.etihad.ae*), the national airline of the United Arab Emirates, was launched in 2003, and is expanding fast.

Most visitors will arrive at **Dubai International Airport** (*Tel: 216 2525. www.dubaiairport.com*), where there are over 90 airlines operating to and from more than 120 destinations. Terminal 1 is used by major airlines, while Terminal 2 is used mainly by airlines serving the former Eastern Bloc countries. A new third terminal at Jebel Ali (Al Maktoum) is used by Emirates Airlines only, and a fourth terminal is being planned. The airport is about 5km (3 miles) northeast of the city centre, and airport buses run every half-hour into the city centre for a fare of Dh3. After a long flight, most prefer the quicker and easier option of taking a taxi direct to their hotel, even though the fare out to the Jumeirah beach hotels is upwards of Dh60.

All signposting is in Arabic and English

By boat

There is a cruise ship terminal at Port Rashid. No ferries operate from Dubai to other countries.

By land

You can drive into Dubai from Oman at the Hatta border post. Sixty-day visas are issued free of charge on the spot to nationals of 33 countries (*see* Passports and Visas, *p152*). Car insurance can be bought at the border and is relatively inexpensive. You can also drive in from any of the other emirates of the United Arab Emirates with no formalities because there are no border controls.

Customs and duty-free

Duty-free allowances are 2 litres (3½ pints) of wine and 2 litres (3½ pints) of spirits for non-Muslims. Two thousand cigarettes, 400 cigars or 2kg (4lb 5oz) of loose tobacco are allowed per person, plus a reasonable amount of perfume. Videos, CDs and DVDs are subject to censorship control, and any items considered pornographic will be confiscated.

Departing

By air

There is no departure tax. Allow some extra time at the airport if you have not completed your present shopping – you can browse in the huge duty-free shop in the departures hall, where there is a range of electrical goods, CDs and DVDs, fashion items and souvenirs, as well as the usual food, alcohol and cigarettes.

By land

Driving out of the country is simple and quick, and the border procedures take no more than a few minutes. If you cross into Oman within 15 days of landing at Dubai Airport, there is no charge for the Omani visa, which otherwise is fairly expensive. Re-entering Dubai after a few days presents no problems and can even be done through a different border post, for example, into Sharjah at Khatmat Malahaw, if that suits your itinerary.

Electricity

Dubai uses the UK-style three-pin plug sockets, so there is no need for adaptors for UK appliances. Those with US or European appliances will need adaptors, but these are cheap and readily available. The voltage is 220V, 50Hz, AC.

Dubai's wealth is conspicuous

Money

The United Arab Emirates dirham (Dh) is divided into 100 fils and notes come in denominations of Dh5, 10, 20, 50, 100, 200, 500 and 1,000. There are only three coins commonly in use: Dh1, and 50 fils and 25 fils.

Exchanging money is easy, and there are exchange bureaux at the airport, all over the city and at the hotels. The currency is pegged to the US dollar.

Exchange bureaux generally give a more competitive rate than banks or hotels. Their opening hours are usually 8.30am–1pm and 4.30–8.30pm. Banks are open Saturday to Wednesday 8am–1pm and Thursday 8am–noon.

ATMs, credit and debit cards

There are ATMs all over the city at banks, shopping malls and hotels. Visa, MasterCard and Amex are widely accepted in shops, hotels and restaurants. Some of the smaller retailers may make an extra charge of 5 per cent for processing a credit card. Traveller's cheques can be exchanged as long as you have your passport with you.

Opening hours

Government departments and embassies. Open: 7.30am–2.30pm.
Businesses. Open: from 8am or 9am to 5pm or 6pm.
Shopping malls. Open: 10am–10pm.
Shops. Most shops shut Friday mornings, reopening from 1pm or 2pm.

Ornate dome at the Ibn Battuta Mall

Friday is the weekly holiday with either Thursday or Saturday tacked on, according to choice.

Passports and visas

Passports must be valid for at least six months from the date of arrival, and they must not show any evidence of an Israeli entry stamp. Compared to most Arab countries, entry into Dubai is straightforward, with 60-day visas issued automatically free of charge on arrival, be it by air, land or sea, to nationals of 33 countries including those of Australia, Canada, most European countries, the UK and the USA. South African nationals have to apply for a visa in advance or can obtain a tourist visa through a local tour operator, which costs Dh100 and lasts 30 days.

Pharmacies

Dubai has many pharmacies all over town, some of which are open 24 hours. Rules about prescription drugs are a lot more lenient than in the West, and most, such as antibiotics, can be bought over the counter. Basic items like painkillers and plasters are stocked by supermarkets and petrol stations.

Post

Stamps are sold at newsagents selling postcards, and there are postboxes at the shopping malls and the big hotels. It costs Dh2 to send a postcard to Australia, Europe and the USA, and delivery is surprisingly slow, taking between one and two weeks to arrive. There is no house delivery in Dubai, so all addresses are PO box numbers.

Public holidays

New Year's Day (1 January), and National Day (2 December) are fixed secular holidays. Christian businesses will take a holiday at Christmas and Easter, but the other public holidays are the Muslim festivals that move according to the lunar calendar. In 2011, 2012 and 2013 these are estimated to be:

26 Nov 2011, 15 Nov 2012, 4 Nov 2013 – Islamic New Year

4 Feb 2012, 24 Jan 2013 – Prophet's Birthday

20 Jul 2012, 9 Jul 2013 – Start of Ramadan

19 Aug 2012, 8 Aug 2013 – Eid Al-Fitr (Feast of the Breaking of the Fast)

6 Nov 2011, 26 Oct 2012, 15 Oct 2013 – Eid Al-Adha (Feast of the Sacrifice)

Suggested reading and media

Dubai Tales by Muhammad Al-Murr (Reed Business Information, 1991) and *From Rags to Riches* by Muhammad Al-Fahim (LCAS, 1995) are two of the very rare books translated into English and written by Emiratis that give insights into local lives.

Oman Trekking Explorer is a booklet that gives detailed routes and maps for hiking. The *Offroad Explorer* booklet also gives information on hiking routes.

The best English daily papers are *Khaleej Times* and *Gulf News*. There is a monthly *Time Out Dubai* and a *What's On*, both of which give thorough listings.

All hotels have satellite television with a full range of news channels, like CNN and BBC World, movie channels and sitcoms. There are two Dubai English-language radio stations, Channel 4 and Dubai Eye, both rather unexciting, which play a mixture of music and give local news and traffic updates.

Tax

Dubai is a tax-free environment, and red tape is kept to a minimum. This keeps prices low and encourages investment. There is no income tax payable on earnings or on rentals, a policy which aims to keep people investing in property here.

Medical facilities in Dubai are excellent

Telephones

Landline to landline calls within Dubai are free, and the telecommunications network is run by the state telecoms company Etisalat. You can direct dial to over 170 countries, after first dialling *00* for an international line. The United Arab Emirates country code for incoming calls is *971*. Within the United Arab Emirates, the area code for Dubai is *04*. There are pay phones all over the city, requiring pre-paid phone cards that you can buy at supermarkets and grocers.

Mobile phones

Dubai's mobile system is GSM (Global System for Mobile), and local numbers begin with *050*. Foreign mobiles will work because there are multiple roaming agreements, but the cost of using your mobile abroad is high. If you plan to use it a lot, it may be worth buying a pre-paid SIM card from Etisalat, known as Wasel GSM. The initial cost is Dh185 with Dh10 of credit, and top-up credit can then be bought from supermarkets and other stores in denominations of Dh30 and Dh60. Using SMS (Short Message Service) texting is much cheaper.

Internet

There are many Internet cafés, and the cost is Dh5–Dh10 an hour. There are an increasing number of Wi-Fi hotspots that you can log into with your laptop at the airport, and in restaurants and coffee shops. Censorship is practised on sites that are considered immoral or pornographic, so anything of that sort will be blocked by the server. Hotels have business centres where guests can log on, and many now have Wi-Fi Internet connections in the room for those travelling with laptops.

Time

Dubai is four hours ahead of GMT (Greenwich Mean Time) with no change from winter to summer timings. It gets dark between 6pm and 7pm all year round.

Toilets

Public toilets do not really exist in Dubai, so you will need to use the facilities at hotels and restaurants, which are generally immaculate. Petrol stations can be used if desperate.

Travellers with disabilities

The airport has excellent facilities with electric buggies, and a few of the taxis can take folded-up wheelchairs. Some of the hotels have dedicated rooms and good access for wheelchair users (*see Directory*), though on the whole the access in towns and in restaurants is not very good. Shopping malls all have disabled parking spaces.

Useful websites

www.godubai.com
www.datadubai.com
www.dubaicityguide.com

With no daylight saving time, the sun starts to set at around 6pm all year round

Language

Signposting in Dubai is bilingual, in Arabic and English. Although Arabic is the official language, in practice English is the most widely used, followed by Hindi and Urdu. The dominance of the non-Arabic speaking population is such that nationals who only speak Arabic often find themselves unable to communicate in their own country in places like hospitals, clinics and shops. Dubai is certainly not the place for budding Arabists to come and practise, and the only place you are likely to hear Arabic is on the local Arabic television channels. Ninety per cent of shopkeepers and assistants are Indian.

A few simple Arabic words and phrases are given below, which in all honesty you will probably only use when travelling in the interior or in neighbouring Oman. The capital letters represent the emphatic letters.

English	Arabic
hello, welcome	*marHaba, ahlan*
goodbye	*ma'a as-salaama*
yes	*aiwa, na'am*
no	*laa*
please	*min faDlak*
sorry, excuse me	*'afwan, muta'assif*
thank you	*shukran*
more, again, also	*kamaan*
is it possible? may I?	*mumkin?*
how much (does it cost?)	*bikaam?*
cheap	*rakhees*
expensive	*ghaalee*
money	*fuluus*

English	Arabic
a lot, much, very	*katheer*
no problem	*mush mushkila*
never mind	*ma'a laysh*
shop	*dukkan*
open	*maftuuH*
shut	*mughlag*
bank	*bank, maSraf*
post office	*maktab bareed*
chemist	*Saydalia*
diarrhoea	*is-haal*
ill, sick	*mareeD*
market	*souk*
museum	*matHaf*
hospital	*mustashfaa*

English	Arabic
police	*buulees*
airport	*maTaar*
ticket	*tadhkara*
suitcase	*shanTa*
hotel	*fundug, ootel*
room	*ghurfa*
toilet, bathroom	*Hammam*
towel	*manshafa*
soap	*Saaboon*
men's	*rijaal*
women's	*sayyidaat*
the bill	*al-Hisaab*
restaurant	*maT'am, restoran*
breakfast	*fuToor*
lunch	*ghadaa*
dinner	*'ashaa*
glass	*kubbeyah*
wine	*khamr, nabeedh*
beer	*beera*
mineral water	*maa ma'daniya*
coffee	*gahwa*
tea	*shay*
today	*al-yawm*
tomorrow	*bukra*
taxi	*taksee*
car	*sayyaara*
petrol	*benzene*

English	Arabic
right	*yameen*
left	*yasaar*
where?	*Wayn?*
what?	*Shuu?*
forbidden	*mamnoo'*
good	*zain*
bad	*mush zain*
hot	*Haar*
cold	*baarid*

Greetings and phrases

The formal greeting on first meeting is: *As-salaamu 'alaykum*, literally, 'May peace be upon you', to which the set reply is: *Wa'alaykum as-salaam*, meaning, 'And on you the peace.'

In sha Allah, meaning 'If God wishes', is used constantly in Arabic about any future arrangement, in the sense of 'hopefully'. It can also be a polite way of avoiding commitment, conveying 'Let us hope so...'

Al-Hamdoo lillah, meaning 'Praise be to God', expresses relief and gratitude every time something works out the way it should have done.

Emergencies

Telephone numbers

Ambulance: *998/999*
Fire: *997*
Police: *999*
Operator: *181*

Health

No vaccinations are required, and Dubai is a safe and healthy place. The biggest risks are from high-speed car accidents, and from the sun and heat. The advice is to drive carefully, away from the main highways, keep out of the midday sun, drink lots of water, wear a sun hat, and use a high-factor suncream. Medical standards are high but treatment is expensive, so make sure you have adequate insurance.

Medical services

Dubai Hospital has a 24-hour emergency department.
Abu Baker Al-Siddiq Road, Hor al-Anz. Tel: 219 5000. www.dohms.gov.ae

Crime and safety

Crime rates are low and the city is quite heavily policed. Pickpocketing in the souk areas is something to be aware of, so keep your wallet well guarded.

Police

For visitors, the Department for Tourist Security acts as a liaison between you and the police. The free number to call if you have a problem is *Tel: 800 4438* and the police website is *www.dubaipolice.gov.ae*

Embassies and consulates

Australia (consulate)
Level 25, Bur Juman Business Tower, Khalifa Bin Zayed Road. Tel: 508 7100. Email: info@austrade.gov.au

Canada (consulate)
7th floor, United Bank Building, Khalid Bin Al-Waleed Road, Bur Dubai. Tel: 352 1717.

New Zealand (consulate)
Suite 1502, API Tower, Sheikh Zayed Road. Tel: 331 7500. Email: dubai@nzte.govt.nz

South Africa (consulate)
3rd floor, Sharaf Building, Khalid Bin Al-Waleed Road, near BurJuman, Bur Dubai. Tel: 397 5222. Email: consul@southafrica.ae. http://southafricadubai.com

UK
British Embassy, Al-Seef Street, Bur Dubai. Tel: 309 4444. Email: britemb@emirates.net.ae. http://ukinuae.fco.gov.uk

USA (consulate)
21st floor, Dubai World Trade Centre, Sheikh Zayed Road, Zabeel. Tel: 311 6000. http://dubai.usconsulate.gov

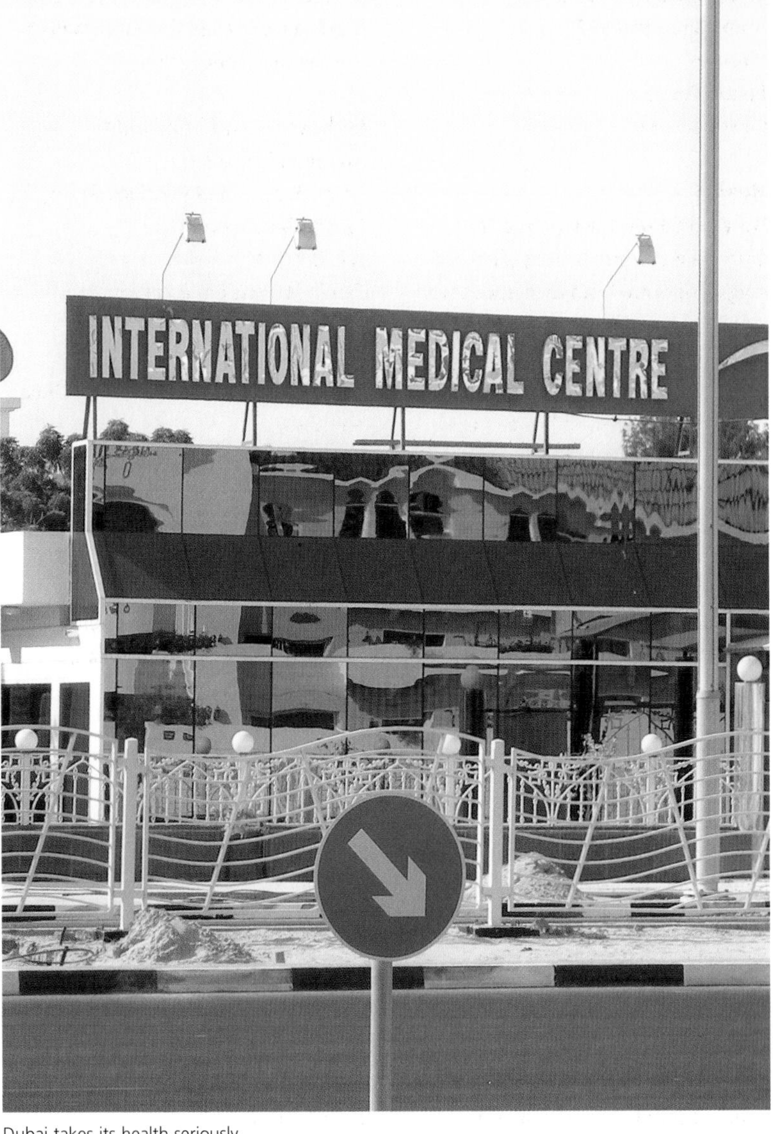

Dubai takes its health seriously

Directory

Accommodation price guide

£ and **££**	Under Dh250
£££	Dh250–Dh500
££££	Dh500–Dh1,000
£££££	Over Dh1,000

Prices of accommodation are based on an average double room for two people sharing, including tax and service.

This price guide gives the full prices quoted by the hotels, although in practice it is rare to pay these as there are always discounts available for one reason or another. If booking direct, always ask for a discount. The price banding reflects the dominance of the four- and five-star establishments. There is far less accommodation at three-star and below as Dubai is catering for the upper end of the market.

Eating out price guide

£ and **££**	Under Dh20
£££	Dh20–Dh40
££££	Dh40–Dh65
£££££	Over Dh65

Prices are based on the average cost of a meal for one from the menu, without drinks.

Alcohol is expensive, and drinking alcohol with your meal can sometimes almost double the cost. All the places listed serve alcohol unless otherwise stated. The price banding reflects the predominance of eateries at the top end of the market. As with the hotels, there are far fewer restaurants towards the lower end. Taxes and service are included.

DUBAI CITY

ACCOMMODATION

Bur Dubai and Deira sides of the Creek

Dubai Youth Hostel £

The best rooms are in the new wing, with simple clean dormitories for four. This is the only real budget accommodation in Dubai, catering for students and backpackers. It does not have good facilities for travellers with disabilities. *Al-Nahda Road beyond the airport. Tel: 298 8151. Email: uaeyha@emirates.net.ae. A bus ride away from the Creek; Bus nos: 3, 13, 17 & 31.*

Al-Hijaz Heritage Motel £££

A simple place with clean rooms in the heart of Deira's heritage and souk area. An old heritage house itself, but not much renovated. Limited wheelchair access. *Next to Al-Ahmadiya School, Deira. Tel: 225 0085. www.alhijazmotel.com*

Four Points Sheraton £££

This hotel is in an ideal location for Dubai's

heritage area and the Gold Souk. It is frequented by businesspeople and has a good Indian restaurant. It does not have adequate facilities for travellers with disabilities. *Khalid Bin Al-Waleed Road, Bur Dubai. Tel: 397 7444. www.fourpoints.com*

Riviera Hotel £££
This makes a great base in old Dubai if you can get one of the Creek-view rooms. Good facilities, but there is limited wheelchair access. *Baniyas Road, Deira. Tel: 222 2131. www.rivierahotel-dubai.com*

XVA £££
One of Dubai's first 'boutique' hotels with just a handful of rooms set around a courtyard in a traditional wind tower house. It is traditionally furnished, with its own art gallery and café. On one floor but no special facilities for travellers with disabilities. *Near Basta Art Café, Bastakia, Bur Dubai. Tel: 353 5383. www.xvagallery.com*

Hilton Dubai Creek ££££
This hotel has fabulous views over the Creek, a rooftop pool, spacious stylish rooms and excellent restaurants – the best hotel on the Creek. There are good facilities for travellers with disabilities. *Baniyas Road, Deira. Tel: 227 1111. Email: reservations.dubai@hilton.com. www.hilton.com*

InterContinental £££££
This has been in its Creekside location on the Deira corniche since 1975, making it one of Dubai's oldest hotels. In 2005 it was refurbished and has now regained some of its prestige. It offers Italian, Japanese and Chinese restaurants, and a seafood one where you pick out your meal and have it cooked specially for you. *Baniyas Road, Deira. Tel: 701 1111. www.intercontinental.com*

Sheraton Dubai Creek Hotel & Towers £££££
With its prime location directly on the Deira side of the Creek shortly before the dhow wharfage and Maktoum Bridge, most of this hotel's 255 rooms have wonderful Creek views. It has Japanese, Italian and Indian restaurants, all of which are first-rate. *Baniyas Road, Deira. Tel: 228 1111. www.sheraton.com/dubai*

Dubai Creek and Downtown

Hyatt Regency £££££
All 400 newly refurbished rooms have views of the sea and the Palm Deira, though there are no beach facilities. As well as its many longstanding and popular restaurants, including Dubai's only revolving one, Al-Dawaar, the hotel also boasts an attached mall with cinemas and ice rink. Good disabled facilities. *Corniche Road, Deira. Tel: 209 1234. www.dubai.regency.hyatt.com*

Shangri-La Hotel £££££
Towering on the Sheikh Zayed Road with its 43 storeys, this excellent hotel has 301 rooms with superb views, two pools, health club and spa and a wide range of

restaurants and bars. It also has 126 serviced apartments suitable for longer stays.
Sheikh Zayed Road. Tel: 343 8888. www.shangri-la.com

Eating out

Al-Mallah £
Experience pavement eating on this busy street where you can watch life go by. Excellent simple *shawarma* (spit-roasted lamb in pitta bread), falafel and fruit juice. No alcohol.
Diyafah Street, Satwa. Tel: 398 4723.

Kan Zaman ££
Right on the Creek promenade, this place is a firm favourite with locals and visitors, especially in the evenings. Serving traditional Arabic food with freshly made bread, it also offers some Emirati dishes not usually found on menus. There is some inside seating with air conditioning for daytime eating out of the sun. No alcohol.
Heritage and Diving Village, Shindagha. Tel: 393 9913.

Antique Bazaar £££
Stylish Indian restaurant furnished with Indian antiques and a colonial atmosphere. There is attentive service and an excellent selection of vegetarian dishes and biryanis.
Four Points Sheraton Hotel, Bur Dubai. Tel: 397 7444. www.fourpoints.com

Après £££
Dubai's very own après-ski lodge set beside the ski slope within the shopping mall. The large open fire completes the Swiss-chalet ambience and the fondue sharing, steaks and pasta make eating here a relaxing experience after a hard day's shopping or skiing.
Mall of the Emirates, Al-Barsha. Tel: 341 4747. www.skidxb.com

Biella Café Pizzeria Ristorante £££
Charming Italian bistro with dining inside or outside in a leafy courtyard. Very popular for lunch with shoppers and businessmen. Good range of pizzas and pasta, with fine seafood dishes. No alcohol.
Wafi Mall, Umm Hurair. Tel: 324 4666. www.wafi.com

Majaz £££
Set within the Aviation Club near Garhoud Bridge, this is reckoned to be the best place for smoking shisha in Dubai. The Lebanese starters are excellent, although the main courses are pretty standard. At night, there is live Arabic music and outdoor eating in the attractive leafy courtyard of Century Village.
Aviation Club, Century Village, Garhoud. Tel: 282 9952. www.aviationclub.ae

Mays El-Reem £££
Cleverly designed Arabic restaurant within the Marriott Hotel, made to feel like a traditional village with ox-carts of fresh fruit and spices. The meze are reasonably priced, and the intimate atmosphere is improved by gentle *oud* (Arabic lute) music. There is freshly baked bread from the oven.
JW Marriott Hotel, Deira. Tel: 607 7977.

Yum! £££
This relaxed restaurant offers a blend of Chinese, Japanese, Thai and Vietnamese cuisine. There is an open kitchen where you can watch your food being prepared, and there are generous portions of noodles. Good for lunch in a casual, modern setting.
Hotel Intercontinental, Creekside, Deira. Tel: 390 4700.

The Boardwalk ££££
A firm favourite because of its amazing location on a wooden platform on stilts over the Creek, this place is wonderful in the winter months for lunch or dinner. International food is served, with a good range of starters, salads, seafood and vegetarian dishes. There are no advance reservations.
Dubai Creek Golf and Yacht Club, Garhoud. Tel: 295 6000. www.dubaigolf.com

Sphinx ££££
Set within the Pyramids of the Wafi Centre, this exotic restaurant has hand-painted Egyptian murals and hieroglyphics for décor, and serves high-class European food. The Friday brunch buffet is good value. There is a small balcony for outdoor eating in the winter months.
Wafi Centre, Umm Hurair. Tel: 324 0000. www.wafi.com

Café Arabesque £££££
This elegantly furnished Arabic restaurant has an attractive view over the Creek. There is a superb range of meze arranged over four tables, representing Lebanon, Syria, Turkey and Jordan. The seats are comfortable, and the ambience is excellent for a special occasion.
Hyatt Regency Hotel, Creekside, Deira. Tel: 317 2222. www.dubai.regency.hyatt.com

Verre £££££
Gordon Ramsay's first restaurant outside the UK, reckoned to be one of the chicest places in town, with superb innovative food and prices to match. There is excellent service with exotic canapés and between-course palate cleansers. Simple, sleek décor.
Hilton Creek Hotel, Deira. Tel: 227 1111. www.gordonramsay.com/dubai

Entertainment

Al-Mansour (Dinner cruise)
A two-hour dhow cruise with international buffet, live Arabic music and shisha (water-pipe).
Radisson SAS, Deira Creek. Tel: 222 7171.

Basta Art Café
In a restored building with an authentic garden ambience and wicker tables and chairs, this café offers healthy meals and chic salads with a children's menu and excellent juices. The art on the walls is for sale.
Bastakia, Bur Dubai. Tel: 353 5071.

Bateaux Dubai (Dinner cruise)
Top-of-the-range modern glass-topped boats offering a superb five-star experience of intimate Creek dining with three-course meals. There is a baby grand piano for gentle background music.

Near British Embassy, Bur Dubai. Tel: 399 4994. www.bateauxdubai.com

Cinestar Gold Cinemas
These Gold Class cinema screens are Dubai's ultimate cinema experience, with fully reclining seats arranged in pairs with a shared private table, adjustable footrests and exquisite snacks. After this level of pampering, it can be difficult to readjust to a standard cinema. There are 11 screens.
Mall of the Emirates, Interchange Four. Tel: 341 4222. www. malloftheemirates.com

Dubai Community Theatre & Arts Centre
Set within the Mall of the Emirates on the upper floor, this is the region's first community-based non-profit-making arts centre, offering theatre, ballet, art, singing and photography. It hosts international performances and also encourages Arabic arts and culture, involving local artists wherever possible.
Mall of the Emirates, Al-Barsha. Tel: 541 4445. www.ductac.org

Irish Village (Pub)
Firm favourite with expats wanting fish and chips (in Guinness® batter) washed down with Dubai's best selection of draught ales and beers. Inside, there are dark beams and alcoves; outside, there are benches on the cobbled yard.
Aviation Club, Garhoud. Tel: 282 4750. www.aviationclub.ae

Issimo (Bar)
Shades of James Bond, with black leather and silver chrome, in this futuristic long narrow bar with Japanese chic. Serves expensive cocktails and there are Swing dance lessons on Saturday nights.
Hilton Creek Hotel, Deira. Tel: 227 1111. www1.hilton.com

Jimmy Dix (Nightclub)
Lively, friendly bar and nightclub with very good grills, burgers, sausages and mash, and even crumbles. There is a relaxed dress code, a live band and a DJ. Regular Thursday Thump weekend parties.
Mövenpick Hotel, Bur Dubai. Tel: 336 8800. www.moevenpick-hotels.com

Laughter House (Comedy)
On the first Tuesday of the month, this venue offers dinner with a stand-up comedy show by a Liverpool comic who flies in for the night.
Rainbow Room, Aviation Club, Garhoud. Tel: 282 4122. www.aviationclub.ae

Metroplex (Cinema)
One of the old favourites, the Metroplex has eight screens and shows all the latest films in English with Arabic subtitles.
Metropolitan Hotel, Sheikh Zayed Road. Tel: 343 8383.

Oxygen (Nightclub)
Plays a range of music styles depending on the night, with R&B, hip-hop and house. Underground and dimly lit, with generous promotions for ladies on certain nights, complimentary drinks or

even champagne. There is a fine restaurant area with sophisticated dining.
Al Bustan Rotana, Garhoud. Tel: 282 0000. www.rotana.com

QD's (Bar)
A stunning location with the best ambience on the Creek, right on the water's edge. The bar serves interesting stylish snacks like Thai fishcakes, satay chicken skewers and nachos, with a huge range of cocktails. There is live music, and shisha, very popular with sundowners.
Dubai Creek Golf and Yacht Club, Garhoud. Tel: 295 6000. www.dubaigolf.com

Studio One (Bar)
An elegant, classy bar with good food and reasonable prices – a popular place where you need a reservation.
Hilton Jumeirah, Dubai Marina. Tel: 399 1111. www1.hilton.com

Tour Dubai (Dinner cruise)
With five traditional dhows of varying sizes, furnished with authentic low-cushioned seating, you can cruise to Shindagha at the mouth of the Creek and back in two hours. There is an Arabic-style buffet and air conditioning.
Bur Dubai creekside, in front of the British Embassy. Tel: 336 8407. www.tour-dubai.com

Vienna Café
A relaxed European-style café tucked in a corner of the Marriott; a good place to unwind after some souk shopping and sightseeing. Serves light salads and snacks.
JW Marriott Hotel, Deira. Tel: 262 4444. www.marriott.com

Vintage (Bar)
Amazing cheese and wine bar offering an enormous range from basic to ultra vintage. The small bar is very popular at weekends when there are fondue evenings.
Pyramids, Wafi Centre, Umm Hurair. Tel: 324 4100. www.wafi.com

Sport and leisure

Al Badia Golf Club
Designed by Robert Trent Jones II, this par 72 course has 11 lakes and is Dubai's latest addition to the golfing scene. The salt-resistant grass can be irrigated with sea water.
Festival City, Ras Al-Khor. Tel: 285 5772. www.albadiagolfclub.ae

Al Boom Diving
This is a purpose-built school with its own fully equipped shop, linked to the PADI (Professional Association of Diving Instructors) Gold Palm Resort at Le Méridien near Fujairah.
Near the Iranian Hospital, Al-Wasl Road. Tel: 342 2993. www.alboomdiving.com

Arabian Ranches Golf Club
An 18-hole course, par 72 and 7,698 yards, with colonial-style Spanish clubhouse and panoramic terrace overlooking the course. Golf Academy with excellent practice facilities. Eleven guest rooms with lovely views.
Emirates Road, PO Box 36700. Tel: 366 3000. www.arabianranches golfdubai.com

Aviation Club (Aerobics and fitness classes)
Garhoud. Tel: 282 4122. www.aviationclub.ae

Balloon Adventures Dubai (Hot-air ballooning)
Two of the largest and most high-tech balloons in the world, with a capacity of 40 people.
Next to the Claridge Hotel, Deira. Tel: 285 4949. www.ballooning.ae. Open: Oct–May, early morning take-off to catch the sunrise.

Cleopatra's Spa
Pampering Egyptian-style with whirlpool, sauna and plunge pool. Massages, facials and anti-ageing treatments. The atmosphere is one of Zen-like calm.
Pyramids, Wafi Centre, Umm Hurair. Tel: 324 7700. www.wafi.com

Dubai Creek Golf & Yacht Club
Recently refurbished, with the first nine holes redesigned by Thomas Bjorn. There is a floodlit driving range and extensive practice facilities.
Garhoud. Tel: 295 6000. www.dubaigolf.com

Emirates Diving Association
This non-profit organisation exists to conserve and protect the United Arab Emirates corals and marine resources. It organises regular clean-up campaigns.
Heritage and Diving Village, Shindagha. Tel: 393 9390. www.emiratesdiving.com

Emirates Equestrian Centre (Horse riding)
Excellent facilities with 147 horses and an international-size floodlit arena. There are lessons for all ages and standards and regular gymkhanas.
Nad Al Sheba. Tel: 553 7986. www.emiratesequestrian centre.com

Emirates Golf Club
Two 18-hole championship courses, one designed by Nick Faldo. The club hosts the annual Dubai Desert Classic. There are extensive practice areas.
Emirates Hills. Tel: 380 1234. www.dubaigolf.com

Galleria Ice Rink
In the middle of the Galleria shopping mall, attached to the Hyatt Regency Hotel. Lessons are available.
Hyatt Regency Hotel, Deira. Tel: 209 6550.

Pharaoh's Club (Climbing, aerobics and fitness classes)
The climbing wall at the Pharaoh's Club has a variety of routes, with crash mats, and lessons with six learners per instructor (adults and children, all levels).
Pyramids, Wafi Centre. Tel: 324 0251. www.wafi.com

Ras Al-Khor Wildlife Sanctuary (Birdwatching)
Dubai's only nature reserve within the city, excellent for flamingos and other waders.
Tel: 206 4240. www.wildlife.ae

Ski Dubai
There are five slopes here at all levels, with a chairlift and drag-lifts. Lessons include equipment hire.
Mall of the Emirates. Tel: 409 4000. www.skidxb.com

Voyagers Xtreme (Hot-air ballooning)
Daily flights in small balloons. You can fly over the city from either Dubai Internet City or Fossil Rock, weather permitting.
Dune Centre, Satwa. Tel: 345 4504.

JUMEIRAH, UMM SUQEIM AND THE SUBURBS

ACCOMMODATION

Jebel Ali Golf Resort & Spa ££££
A tranquil resort hotel on its own private beach set in 52ha (128 acres) of beautifully landscaped gardens well away from the city. It has its own golf course, marina, spa, horse riding centre, shooting and watersports. Good facilities for travellers with disabilities.
Jebel Ali. Tel: 883 6000. www.jebelali-international.com. Email: jagrstrev@jaihotels.com

Le Méridien Mina Seyahi Resort ££££
This resort has 211 spacious rooms overlooking the sea, one of the longest stretches of private beach in Dubai, and its own marina with a range of watersports. There is a Penguin Club for children, and a Barasti Bar on the beach. The gardens are lushly landscaped. Limited facilities for travellers with disabilities.
Al-Sufouh Road, Jumeirah. Tel: 399 3333. www.lemeridien-minaseyahi.com

Burj Al-Arab Hotel £££££
This ultimate Dubai icon has to be mentioned even though few will be able to afford its sky-high prices. Its 202 suites are all duplex with internal staircases, and guests tend to be celebrities. Even access is restricted and you will not be allowed through the barrier onto the artificial island without a reservation. Good facilities for travellers with disabilities.
Jumeirah Road, Jumeirah. Tel: 301 7777. www.burj-al-arab.com

Dubai Marine Beach Resort & Spa £££££
This independent beach hotel is the closest one to the city centre, with 195 villa-style rooms spread among beautifully lush and landscaped gardens, complete with waterfalls and streams. Scattered around the extensive grounds are three pools, a health club and a spa. There is a small private beach.
Jumeirah Beach Road, Jumeirah. Tel: 346 1111. www.dxbmarine.com

Jumeirah Beach Hotel £££££
After Burj Al-Arab Hotel, this is Dubai's most distinctive landmark hotel, designed in the shape of a wave. The interior is very striking and colourful, and all 618 rooms have sea views. There are beautifully landscaped grounds with a private beach and pool, and excellent sports facilities. The superb location is beside the Wild Wadi Waterpark, with views of Burj Al-Arab. There are several restaurants, including one on the beach. Facilities for travellers with disabilities are good.

Jumeirah Road, Jumeirah. Tel: 348 0000. www.jumeirahbeachhotel.com

Mina A'Salam £££££

One of the two hotels within this beautifully designed Arabian fantasy resort, where the hotels, the old-Arabian-style shopping mall, the spa, and 45 restaurants and cafés are all linked by a series of canals navigated by *abras* (crossing boats). Everything you could possibly want can be found within the resort, and many never venture beyond it. The elegant rooms have balconies with views over the harbour and sea. In total, there are 940 rooms and even some exclusive summer houses. Good facilities for travellers with disabilities.
Al-Sufouh Road, Jumeirah. Tel: 366 8888. www.madinatjumeirah.com

One & Only Royal Mirage £££££

This magnificent resort has an intimate atmosphere with traditional Islamic architecture and excellent Moroccan cuisine. There are three separate establishments: The Palace, Arabian Court and Residence & Spa. The nightclub is called Kasbar, with very stylish Arabian décor.
Al-Sufouh Road, Jumeirah. Tel: 399 9999. www.oneandonlyresorts.com

Ritz-Carlton £££££

This exclusive 138-room hotel is low rise and has an elegant Mediterranean feel. All rooms have a sea view and their own balcony or patio. The Lobby Lounge offers wonderful afternoon tea with scones, and the gardens are beautifully landscaped with fine swimming pools.
Dubai beach, opposite the Marina, Jumeirah. Tel: 399 4000. www.ritzcarlton.com

Eating out

Automatic £

An excellent chain that has been going for 25 years, serving good Arabic food. There is a huge range of meze and good-size portions of fish and kebabs. The staff are friendly and the décor is clean, bright and minimalist. No alcohol.
Beach Centre, Jumeirah. Tel: 349 4888.

Reem Al-Bawadi £££

Traditionally decorated Arabic restaurant, this place is always busy because of its reputation for good food and shisha (water-pipe) areas where you can loll on low cushions smoking before or after eating. There are some local specialities not found in other places. No alcohol.
Close to the HSBC bank, Beach Road, Jumeirah. Tel: 394 7444.

BiCE ££££

This serves a wonderful mix of Italian food and nouvelle cuisine. There is a great atmosphere with live piano music, 1930s Art Deco and windows overlooking the pool. The restaurant is very popular and has an extensive wine list.
Hilton Jumeirah Hotel, Dubai Marina. Tel: 399 1111. www.hilton.com

The Dhow ££££

Permanently moored traditional dhow

specialising in seafood with fresh oysters, sushi and sashimi. The top deck dining is alfresco and the lower deck is air-conditioned.
Le Méridien Mina Seyahi, Al-Sufouh.
Tel: 399 3333.

Malecon ££££
A Cuban restaurant with wonderful views over the Dubai marine lagoon. Salsa dancers and live music complement the excellent paella and provide a sultry ambience late at night. Children are welcome earlier in the evening.
Dubai Marine Beach, Beach Road, Jumeirah.
Tel: 346 1111.
www.dxbmarine.com

Zheng He's £££££
Probably Dubai's classiest Chinese restaurant, this is in a wonderful waterside spot within the Mina A'Salam Hotel in the Madinat Jumeirah complex. It serves superior cuisine, especially the marinated fish and stir-fry dishes. There is unusual dim sum with exotic dips and sauces, and a large wine list.
Mina A'Salam, Madinat Jumeirah, Umm Suqeim.
Tel: 366 8888. www. madinatjumeirah.com

Entertainment

The Alamo (Bar)
Good all-round bar with quiz nights, ladies' nights, karaoke nights, football nights and live music. A lively atmosphere with a regular crowd of expats.
Dubai Marine Beach, Beach Road, Jumeirah.
Tel: 349 3455.
Open: noon–3am.

Bahri Bar
This is the perfect setting for delicious nibbles and cocktails, with stunning views over the wind towers, canals and palm trees of this superbly designed resort complex.
Mina A'Salam, Madinat Jumeirah.
Tel: 366 8888. www. madinatjumeirah.com

Costa (Café)
Set within the wonderful Italianate Mercato Mall, here you can pretend you are sitting in a Venice pavement café. It serves luxury sandwiches and cakes.
Mercato, Beach Road, Jumeirah.
Tel: 344 5705.

Grand Mercato (Cinema)
With seven screens, this stylish cinema in the Italian Renaissance setting of the Mercato Mall makes a fun night out.
Mercato Mall, Beach Road, Jumeirah.
Tel: 349 9773.
www.grandcinemas.com

Left Bank (Pub)
With its terrace on the canal of the Madinat Jumeirah complex, this contemporary pub is good for lunch with simple meat and fish dishes and an excellent selection of beers and wines.
Souk Madinat Jumeirah, Umm Suqeim.
Tel: 368 6171.

Madinat Theatre
This is an excellent venue for visiting performances. Well designed, with seating for over 400, this theatre offers a full range of theatre from comedies to classics. All part of the complete Madinat Jumeirah complex experience.

Souk Madinat Jumeirah, Umm Suqeim. Tel: 366 6546. www.madinattheatre.com

Sahn Eddar (Café)
An affordable way to peek inside the lavish Burj Al-Arab Hotel (*see p79*), with afternoon tea taken either here in the lobby or upstairs in the Sky View Bar. The exquisite sandwiches, scones, cakes, sweets and chocolate that are on offer will set you up for the whole evening.
Burj Al-Arab, Umm Suqeim. Tel: 301 7600. www.burj-al-arab.com

Trilogy (Nightclub)
On three floors within the Madinat Jumeirah complex, this amazing venue boasts six bars and a capacity of 1,000. The design is stunning, with a *majlis*-style low-cushioned chill-out area. Glitzy but sophisticated, this is the favourite of Dubai's social elite, with special VIP Glass Cages or private lounges for hire.
Souk Madinat Jumeirah, Umm Suqeim. Tel: 366 8888. www.trilogy.ae

Uptown (Bar)
Up on the 24th floor, this bar's outdoor terrace, with views over the Burj Khalifa, is bigger than its interior. Fine cocktails, wines and bottled beers are served, with tasty bar snacks, nuts and nibbles.
Jumeirah Beach Hotel, Umm Suqeim. Tel: 406 8181.

Sport and leisure

Big Apple (Aerobics and fitness classes)
Jumeirah. Tel: 319 8661.

Club Joumana (Horse riding, fishing)
This riding centre has six horses. It gives desert hacks to experienced riders or lessons in the riding school. For the fishing, there are trips with seven people per boat for four or eight hours, complete with captain and provisions. Possible catches are barracuda, grouper, kingfish, lemonfish and trevally.
Jebel Ali Golf Resort and Spa. Tel: 883 6000. www.jebelali-international.com. Closed: during the hot summer months.

The Desert Course (Golf)
Designed by Ian Baker-Finch and Nicklaus Design, the 72-par course has a shop and range of bars and restaurants. The golf carts have GPS (global positioning systems).
Arabian Ranches. Emirates Road 311, PO Box 36700. Tel: 366 3000.

Desert Rangers (Dune Buggy Driving)
Safe safaris in a dune buggy, complete with a barbecue at a desert campsite. Expensive but memorable.
Dubai Garden Centre, Al Quoz. Tel: 422 0044. www.desertrangers.com

Dubai Archers Club
Archery lessons and equipment hire.
Dubai Country Club. Tel: 344 2591. Open: Thur & Fri afternoons.

The Dubai Country Club (Aerobics and fitness classes)
Tel: 333 1155.

Dubai Kite Club (Watersports)
This is the club that regulates kitesurfing in Dubai, as it requires a licence. The only beach where it is permitted is near the old Wollongong University premises.
Mina Seyahi Dubai, Al Sufouh.
Tel: 050 618 0612.
Closed: Fridays.

Dubai Offshore Sailing Club
Sailing lessons for groups or individuals at all levels.
Umm Suqeim Beach.
Tel: 394 1669.
www.dosc.ae

Dubai Polo & Equestrian Club
Lessons in riding, jumping and dressage are available here. Three hundred livery stables, tack shop, and clubhouse with bars and restaurants.
Arabian Ranches, PO Box 7477, Dubai.
Tel: 361 8111.
www.poloclubdubai.com

Dubai Roadsters (Cycling)
Dubai's cycling club has Friday rides of 65–100km (40–62 miles) and weekday rides of 30–50km (18½–31 miles). No membership fees.
Tel: 339 4453.
www.dubairoadsters.com

Jebel Ali Equestrian Club
Qualified instructors give lessons to children and adults, with jumping and dressage. There are desert hacks for experienced riders.
Jebel Ali Village.
Tel: 884 5485.

Montgomerie Golf Club
Designed by Colin Montgomerie, the 18th hole is 600m (656yds) long. The clubhouse has guest rooms, a spa, bars and restaurants.
Emirates Hills.
Tel: 390 5600. www.themontgomerie.com

Pavilion Dive Centre
This PADI (Professional Association of Diving Instructors) Gold Palm Centre is run by PADI course instructors. It organises a variety of courses (at all levels) and dives in Dubai, Khor Fakkan and even Musandam.
Jumeirah Beach Hotel, Beach Road, Jumeirah.
Tel: 406 8828. www.thepaviliondivecentre.com

The Resort Course (Golf)
A nine-hole course, par 36, used for the mini-tournament that precedes the Dubai Desert Classic.
Jebel Ali Golf Resort and Spa.
Tel: 883 6000. www.jebelali-international.com

Talise Wellness Spa
With a wonderful ambience of calm and serenity, this place offers the most extensive range of treatments available in Dubai. It has an oasis feel, with plunge pool, sauna and steam rooms. Yoga classes are also on offer.
Madinat Jumeirah.
Tel: 366 6818.
www.jumeirah.com

DUBAI BEYOND THE CITY

Accommodation

Bab Al-Shams Desert Resort & Spa ££££
Designed like an Arab fort in the desert, the rooms are spacious and furnished in Arabian

style. The pool beside the desert and the exotic Satori Spa will keep adults happy, while there is a kids' club for little ones. International cuisine with traditional open-air Arabian dining. There is wheelchair access.
50km (31 miles) beyond Dubai. Tel: 381 3231. www.meydanhotels.com/babalshams

Hatta Fort Hotel ££££
This exclusive 50-room mountain retreat has chalet-style rooms, each with an outdoor patio. It is set in 32ha (80 acres), with its own pool, golf driving range, floodlit tennis courts, mini-golf, gym, jogging track, trekking routes, archery, clay pigeon shooting and mountain biking. The facilities are not good for travellers with disabilities.
An hour's drive from Dubai, 10 minutes' drive from the Oman border, PO Box 9277, Dubai. Tel: 852 3211. www.jebelali-international.com. Email: hfh@jaihotels.com

Al-Maha Desert Resort & Spa £££££
Dubai's first eco-resort has breeding oryx in its 225sq km (87sq mile) conservation reserve. The suites are detached with tent-style roofs, and each has its own private pool. There are champagne camel rides and private wildlife drives. There is wheelchair access to one suite. No children or casual visitors.
65km (40 miles) outside Dubai. Tel: 252 0222. www.al-maha.com

Eating out

Al-Hadheerah £££££
This is Dubai's authentic open-air Arabic restaurant. Highly atmospheric, it is set around a courtyard with *barasti* (palm frond) walls, throw rugs, rustic furniture and oil lamps. There is a choice of seating from Arabic-style low cushions on the floor, to intimate alcoves with tables and chairs. The food is an Arabic-style buffet with spit roasts and stone ovens. In the evenings there is a belly dancer and live band.
Within the Bab Al-Shams Desert Resort and Spa. 50km (31 miles) beyond Dubai. Tel: 832 6699. www.meydanhotels.com/babalshams

Sport and leisure

Hatta Fort Hotel (Archery)
A 25m (82ft) archery range with eight targets. This is the venue for the Dubai Archers' annual tournament. There is supervised practice.
An hour's drive from Dubai, 10 minutes' drive from the Oman border, PO Box 9277, Dubai. Tel: 852 3211. www.jebelali-international.com

Satori Spa
This beautiful spa treatment centre is on two floors with its own small garden. There is a full range of massages and detox treatments, reflexology and a sanarium (sauna and steam bath combined).
Within the Bab Al-Shams Desert Resort and Spa. 50km (31 miles) beyond Dubai. www.meydanhotels.com/babalshams

Index

Acknowledgements

Thomas Cook Publishing wishes to thank DIANA DARKE, to whom the copyright belongs, for the photographs in this book, except for the following images:

ALAMY 77 (Caro), 110 (Tibor Bognar)
CREATIVEI IMAGES, WWW.SHUTTERSTOCK.COM 115
DREAMSTIME.COM 1 (Ruthblack), 13 (Rubengutierrez), 27 (Ippirolf), 29 (Acitore), 108 (Typhoonski), 113 (Styve), 152 (Steve Rosset), 155 (Billie Muller)
DUBAI TOURISM BOARD 92
FLICKR/Michelangelo Rd 43, bewarenerd 44, daarkfire 49, 96, 103, iapetus11 54, Mamamusings 65, Makz 69, Ericsson Beach 73, Tortoise 75, 122, dopesmuglar 79, One Divine Hammer 83, Lost Bob 86, buckofive 101, travelling runes 112, Guillaume 114, Mathias M 118, Frank Gloystein 146, Blakeisrael 147
WIKIMEDIA COMMONS 102 (Shahin Olakara)
WORLD PICTURES PHOTOSHOT 28, 51, 57

For CAMBRIDGE PUBLISHING MANAGEMENT LIMITED:
Project editor: Ed Robinson
Typesetter: Paul Queripel
Proofreaders: Thomas Willsher & Rachel Norridge

SEND YOUR THOUGHTS TO
BOOKS@THOMASCOOK.COM

We're committed to providing the very best up-to-date information in our travel guides and constantly strive to make them as useful as they can be. You can help us to improve future editions by letting us have your feedback. If you've made a wonderful discovery on your travels that we don't already feature, if you'd like to inform us about recent changes to anything that we do include, or if you simply want to let us know your thoughts about this guidebook and how we can make it even better – we'd love to hear from you.

Send us ideas, discoveries and recommendations today and then look out for your valuable input in the next edition of this title.

Emails to the above address, or letters to the traveller guides Series Editor, Thomas Cook Publishing, PO Box 227, Coningsby Road, Peterborough PE3 8SB, UK.

Please don't forget to let us know which title your feedback refers to!